Autism 24/7

A Family Guide to Learning at Home and in the Community

TOPICS IN AUTISM

Autism 24/7

A Family Guide to Learning at Home and in the Community

Andy Bondy, Ph.D. &
Lori Frost, M.S., CCC/SLP

Sandra L. Harris, Ph.D., series editor

Woodbine House ◆ 2008

Published in the United States of America by Woodbine House, Inc., 6510 Bells Mill Rd., Bethesda, MD 20817. 800-843-7323. www.woodbinehouse.com

Library of Congress Cataloging-in-Publication Data

Bondy, Andy.
Autism 24/7 : a family guide to learning at home and in the community / Andy Bondy and Lori Frost. — 1st ed.
p. cm. — (Topics in autism)
Includes bibliographical references and index.
ISBN 978-1-890627-53-9
1. Autism in children. 2. Autistic children—Care. I. Frost, Lori. II. Title. III. Title: Autism twenty-four/seven.
RJ506.A9B653 2008
618.92'85882—dc22

2007044841

Manufactured in the United States of America

First Edition

10 9 8 7 6 5 4 3 2 1

To the many children, families, and professionals
for the many lessons they've taught us.

In particular, Lori wishes to thank Tom Layton, Ph.D.,
and Andy wishes to thank Marilyn Erickson, Ph.D.,
for their many years of guidance during
our years of graduate training.

Table of Contents

Introduction

When Becky was a year and a half old, she was not interacting with her parents or her brother as expected and she had yet to say a word. Soon, she was formally diagnosed with autism. Now Becky is almost 5 and has been attending an excellent educational program designed to help children with similar educational and developmental needs. The school program is based upon the principles of learning developed within the field of applied behavior analysis. It places a strong emphasis upon developing communication and learning skills typically seen in preschoolers. Becky's parents, George and Myra Engler, are proud that she has made excellent progress at school and pleased with the lessons her teachers have taught her.

George and Myra have studied the teaching strategies recommended by their daughter's school program. They spend many hours each week arranging for Becky to practice the skills taught at school. Despite their daughter's progress, however, including Becky within the normal routines of family life is problematic. Up until now, they have tried to meet Becky's everyday needs directly—often anticipating what she wants, avoiding situations that are stressful to her, and trying to use the materials they've observed the teachers using at school. But weekends are becoming too difficult for the family. Becky does not enjoy noisy, public places such as supermarkets or the mall. She doesn't enjoy watching her older brother play soccer or skateboard. She runs to her room whenever visitors, including relatives, come to the house. Sometimes Myra and George wonder if they are supposed to convert their home into a school so that all routines are familiar and comfortable for Becky.

Myra and George have decided that Becky needs to learn to be a full participating family member and are looking for ways to accomplish this goal. This book is dedicated to families like the Englers who are seeking to help their children with autism and related disabilities fully integrate into the routines of a family within and around the home.

During the past few decades, effective strategies have been developed to help children with autism learn many crucial skills. (See, for example, *Right from the Start by* Sandra Harris and Mary Jane Weiss.) For many young children with autism, learning to communicate with their parents, peers, and teachers is a daunting challenge. Important strides have been made to help these children learn to speak or to use other modalities to communicate. Children with autism often have difficulty in imitating the actions of their parents and siblings. Here, too, great progress has been made in developing strategies to teach imitation, and then to use this new skill to acquire other skills.

Still, Becky has difficulties with communication and imitation skills. She also has problems in acquiring skills everyone thinks of as "natural" for toddlers and preschoolers—playing with toys, engaging in imaginative play with friends, acting as "mommy's little helper" when she is doing common household chores, and learning to have fun out in the community. Going into her neighborhood— whether to shop, visit doctors and other specialists, or play in the park—has become a stressful event for her and everyone in the family. Most children seem to enjoy "free time," but Becky spends it in ways that often lead to serious behavior problems or "shutting down" in a manner that is difficult to get her out of. Sometimes, moving from room to room or activity to activity, or simply changing who is currently taking care of her causes Becky to loudly protest.

If your child is like Becky, your family may be experiencing some or all of the same frustrations related to integrating your child into your family life. If your child is older, you may have other difficulties, perhaps related to delays in acquiring self-help skills. You may worry that, unless your child masters these skills, she will continue to need intensive parental involvement, thus limiting the extent to which she will be able to enjoy her adult years.

This book is designed to help all families of children with autism spectrum disorders overcome the challenges that keep their family life from running as smoothly as they would like. In the next chapters, we will provide examples of how George and Myra, and the families of other children with autism and related disabilities, can:

- effectively teach their children to participate in important as well as routine family activities at home and in the neighborhood;
- select appropriate skills associated with the routines of home life as well as communication and social skills;
- learn how best to use a variety of strategies, including many that are visually based, to help children communicate and to better understand our efforts to communicate with them;
- learn how we can help motivate children to learn often complex lessons while participating in home- and community-based routines;
- alter and expand goals over time so that the children can continue to demonstrate new skills. To accomplish these goals, we will describe teaching strategies that parents and other family members can successfully use with their children;
- minimize errors over time, since all learners occasionally make mistakes.

Our hope is that we can show that it not necessary for parents to convert their homes into a school. We are confident that children with autism spectrum disorders can effectively learn in all parts of the home as well as in the most common and important aspects of their neighborhoods—from stores to playgrounds. We will use many real-life examples to help make our suggestions as real and practical as possible.

The Pyramid Approach to Education

As the statewide director of a public school program for students with autism, the first author needed a strategy to organize the factors that teachers, specialists, and parents required to develop effective educational environments both in and out of school. The strategy developed to meet this need—the Pyramid Approach to Education—has been successfully applied within numerous classrooms on an international scale. (See *The Pyramid Approach to Education in Autism* by A. Bondy and B. Sulzer-Azaroff, 2002, for a detailed description.) One indication of its success is the recognition received by the Sussex Consortium, which is part of the statewide Delaware Autism Program. With its complete implementation of the Pyramid model, this program received the 2002 Wendy F. Miller Autism Program of the Year Award in recognition of its excellence by the Autism Society of America (ASA).

The Pyramid Approach integrates broad-spectrum behavior analysis with a heavy emphasis upon functional communication. It provides a problem-solving strategy that school staff and parents can follow, both to achieve effective learning and to address common problems related to either challenging behaviors or slow acquisition of skills.

The shape of a pyramid is used to help address particular issues in an organized fashion. As with the construction of a real pyramid, we begin with certain issues at the base of the pyramid and gradually build our way up to form a well-balanced, solid model. The foundation of the Pyramid relates to the principles of learning first espoused by psychologist B.F. Skinner and demonstrated within the field of applied behavior analysis. Skinner stressed that the most important aspect of behavior is how it is functionally related to the environment. He studied how events that happen before (antecedents) and after (consequences) a behavior can influence the likelihood that the behavior will occur again or change in some way.

Next, the four base struts of the Pyramid deal with issues associated with "What to teach." These topics include:

a. a focus on functional skills and objectives in many different environments,
b. motivational factors, with a stress on using powerful reinforcement systems,
c. functional communication skills and critical social skills, and
d. challenging behaviors, which we refer to as "contextually inappropriate behaviors."

Once these core issues are in place, then we turn our attention to issues related to "How to teach." These factors are organized around four key areas:

a. generalization, which includes systematically planning to assure that the student can apply various skills in a broad and sustainable fashion,

b. designing effective lessons that may differ in terms of their simplicity or sequence or in terms of whether they are teacher- vs. student-led,
c. teaching strategies that may involve the use of prompts and how to eliminate them, as well as how to use feedback alone ("shaping") to achieve learning, and
d. planning to minimize errors and knowing how to react when the student makes errors.

Finally, we evaluate the effectiveness of our efforts and thus must address issues related to data collection and analysis.

It is important to understand that when this model is taught, everyone—regardless of their personal, educational, or teaching history—learns its elements and how to implement them in the same sequence. That is, staff and parents essentially undergo the same training, although the professional training of many staff will permit a deeper analysis of certain issues. The goal is to permit school personnel and parents to communicate with each other in a manner that will yield the most effective teaching environments for the children with whom we are all concerned.

How This Book Is Organized

We have organized the topics in this book to follow the basic sequence of questions posed by the Pyramid Approach. We will try to avoid overwhelming readers with highly technical terms or jargon, although we will use specific language to help clarify certain points. This book will not cover the contents of the Pyramid Approach in depth—for that goal, please refer to the book previously cited by Bondy & Sulzer-Azaroff. You may also wish to refer to the study guide that accompanies that book (*Study Questions, Laboratory, and Field Activities to Accompany the Pyramid Approach to Education in Autism*, Sulzer-Azaroff, Fleming & Mashikian, 2003).

This book will explore issues that parents like the Englers can take advantage of to successfully teach their children skills that are important at home and in their neighborhood. We will point out that while teachers and parents may use similar teaching strategies, there are aspects of home and community that are unique and that offer special opportunities when working on important skills. These skills will include many functional ones that children need to become competent and independent while living at home, as well as skills needed to successfully navigate in the outside world.

We will first consider factors that will help parents choose goals that are reasonable and attainable, both in and around the home. We then will describe ways to help motivate your child to learn skills that you have found to be important. Some children with autism spectrum disorders may be able to actively help choose what is important for them to learn, but there will be times when you will need to help convince your child that a skill you pick is truly important! We will then focus on communication and social skills that will have lifelong influences regarding how your child interacts with people within your family and the community at large. Next, we will look at the many opportunities available within your home to help create effective lessons that will last throughout your child's life. We will continue with a discussion of teaching strategies that can be used by parents and other family members, and then focus on ways to react when our children make mistakes or simply don't do what we expect them to do. Since no one can guarantee that a particular teaching strategy will work, we will review ways that parents can collect information that will help them evaluate the effectiveness of their lessons. Finally, we will take an extensive look at how your child can best achieve the skills necessary to integrate into the neighborhood and community.

It is our firm belief, backed by our experience and considerable research performed by scores of people over many years, that children with autism spectrum disorders live most successfully and happily at home and in the community when they are engaged in functional activities, have a clear system of reinforcement in place, and have support for their communication skills, both expressive and receptive. When these three critical factors are in place, significant behavior management problems are greatly reduced and children learn new skills in ways that are efficient, practical, and enduring.

1 Setting Goals at Home

Kris was a school psychologist at a renowned public school program for children with autism. He was very sensitive to the stress levels of parents and felt confident that if he could reduce stress, then the children were more likely to show the skills they had acquired at school in all settings. Kris was comfortable with the goals that teachers and specialists typically recommended for the very young, incoming students—orienting to the teachers and their instructions, improving their communication skills, and reducing the inappropriate behaviors they often had when they entered the school program.

Kris typically interviewed parents about the impact their child had on their home life. While interviewing Amy and Mark Baskel about their typical grocery shopping patterns, he was surprised to learn of a style he had never dreamt of. They calmly told him that one of them would usually shop at one o'clock in the morning. Kris asked if this had anything to do with special sales at that hour. The parents said that they picked that hour because one of them could shop while the other stayed home, most confident that their three-year old son, Billy, would be asleep! Kris then asked if they had considered taking their son to the grocery store with them. They looked at each other, and then simply laughed. A few weeks later, Kris asked the classroom staff to take Billy to the supermarket. Upon their return, they told Kris about Billy's loud tantrums throughout their trip to the store and exclaimed that they now understood why the Baskels had laughed—and that they now knew a critical skill for Billy to learn.

How Do We Choose What to Focus On?

How do we help parents determine what's important to teach to their children at home and in their neighborhood? As we can see from the above example, teaching Billy to accompany his parents to the supermarket would permit them to shop at a more normal hour, and also greatly reduce their stress levels. So, one important way to determine what we should teach is to identify what typical family patterns are most disrupted and thus lead to substantial stress for all members of the family.

The other major way to pinpoint what we should teach is to determine what skills are most important for a child to learn so he can become less dependent on adults. When children are very young, parents and other caregivers expect to do many things and provide great support for these family members. But as children grow, we increasingly expect them to participate more fully in many routines at home and in the neighborhood. If this change does not occur, parents' levels of involvement remain very high. So, you will want to consider the various ways that your child's lack of skills leads to additional stress relative to what you would expect of other children at the same age. For example, if your teenage son cannot help in any of the laundry routine, then you will be spending many extra hours every week doing his laundry, just as you did when he was two years old.

On the other hand, you may experience stress because of the disruptive behavior your child displays either at home or in neighborhood settings. In our example above, while Billy's parents would not expect a great deal of independence from any three-year-old in a supermarket, they were concerned with the tantrums they had to deal with when they took their son shopping with them. As we shall discuss in Chapter 7 on "Dealing with Difficult Behaviors," sometimes a problematic behavior is related to your child's lack of skill in some area, but other times your child may well have a skill but not use it in certain situations.

Your first step, therefore, in figuring out how to improve your family life is to consider critical areas in which your child either has:

a. limited skills, or
b. significant problem behaviors that you feel cause ongoing stress within your family.

For issues that involve skills related to communication, please refer to Chapter 3 for more details about functional communication goals.

We've provided the form below (Table 1-1) for you to fill in with other members of your family. We suggest you limit your answer to three or four items in each category so that you will be able to create a workable list of goals. Right now, we are only concerned with finding areas that are causing stress within the family. Later, we will describe how you may best work on teaching certain skills (Chapter 5) and handle behavior management problems (Chapter 7).

Table 1-1 | Skill Deficits and Problem Behaviors

Location	**Skill Deficit**	**Problem Behavior**
At home	Example: *Cannot tie shoes* 1. 2. 3.	Example: *Screams for help* 1. 2. 3.
Neighborhood	Example: *Cannot cross streets* 1. 2. 3.	Example: *Opens other people's mailboxes* 1. 2. 3.
Community Settings	Example: *Cannot buy snacks independently* 1. 2. 3.	Example: *Runs through the mall* 1. 2. 3.

Other Methods for Determining What to Teach

Focusing on the most stressful situations may seem like a natural way to prioritize what to teach at home. However, your child may not have many problem behaviors or you may feel that his skill deficits interfere with home life more than the presence of problem behaviors. So, in addition to reviewing critical behaviors, you should also look more broadly at important skills to teach. There are two other systematic approaches that will help you discover what you should teach at home. One system relates to the time of day when problems occur, while the other focuses on the area of the house (or the location in the community) where your child experiences difficulties.

The Time-Based Approach

When we follow the time-based approach to identifying skills to teach, we ask parents to describe common sequences of events in the course of the day and then cluster activities by when they occur. For example, what are the routines for school-day mornings? Often, parents will describe a sequence similar to that shown in Table 1-2—

Table 1-2 | Sample Schedule

7:00 AM	Wake Billy
7:03	Take Billy to the bathroom and use toilet
7:07	Go back to bedroom and help Billy take off his pajamas
7:11	Help Billy put on his school clothes and sneakers
7:20	Go to the kitchen and turn on TV with favorite video running
7:23	Eat cereal (without milk!), drink juice, eat 5 grapes while watching TV
7:40	Go to bathroom, wash hands and face, brush teeth
7:50	Go to living room and watch TV (cartoons)
8:05	Get coat and backpack
8:10	Leave house and get on bus

starting with when they wake up their child to the time when he gets on the school bus.

We would continue to ask for a description of other time-chunks, such as:

1. The block of time in the afternoon after the child comes home from school;
2. Times associated with preparing, eating, and cleaning up after dinner;
3. Early evening recreational activities;
4. Preparing for and taking a bath;
5. Getting ready for and going to bed.

Of course, on weekends and holidays, families typically identify other significant blocks of time (see Table 1-3 for examples of common weekend family-based activities). When you make this type of timetable, be certain to indicate whether it relates to everyday or special routines.

Notice that these examples focus on routines at home. It will be helpful to start with a full description of your life at home, but you will eventually want to write down routines for community activities and events. It is possible that your family has a routine or frequent commu-

Table 1-3 | Detailed Schedule for Saturday Mornings

(Make time adjustments for Billy's actual wake-up time.)

7:00 AM	Wake Billy
7:03	Take Billy to the bathroom and use toilet
7:07	Put in Billy's favorite videotape or DVD while he plays in his room in his pajamas
7:45	Help Billy put on his play clothes and sneakers
8:00	Go to the kitchen and turn on TV in kitchen with favorite video running
8:10	Eat cereal (without milk!), drink juice, eat 5 grapes
8:30	Take Billy to bathroom, wash hands and face, brush teeth
8:45	Go to living room and watch TV (cartoons)
9:30	Let Billy wake up Dad and jump on his bed!
9:40	Get Billy to help Mom bring laundry to basement

nity outing on many school nights. These could include visits by tutors or other specialists (e.g., the piano teacher), trips to a dance class, or Scout meetings. For such events, be sure to note the people your child interacts with as well as the activities in which he is expected to participate.

The Area-Based Approach

Another way to identify important skills to teach is to review all areas in and around your home. When we follow the area-based approach, we talk to parents about common activities and routines in particular areas of the house. In addition to asking questions about common expectations for the child, we would ask questions about particular areas of the house that currently cause significant stress. Sometimes these areas are places in the home in which some family members like or need to engage in particular activities that your child does not participate in. For example, if you need to spend time in the kitchen preparing dinner, what will your three-year-old do at the same time?

Table 1-4 includes a list of common areas in a home or apartment and activities that families often do within those areas. Using the blank form provided on page 148, please list the typical activities that members of your family engage in. You may want to make a special note if you expect your child to do something other than what other people are doing. For example, you may be cutting vegetables for dinner but you'd like your child to use a coloring book while sitting at the kitchen table.

Consider what you expect of your child while in the kitchen, the living room, his own bedroom, the basement work-area, and so on. Be sure to consider what you expect your child to do while you are watching TV. Parents may hope that their child will also watch TV, but ask yourself if you should reasonably expect your child to watch the same shows as you do. That is, if Mom likes to watch the 6 o'clock local news, what will she expect her son to do in the living room at that time? Are there toys that he can play with, or are there other recreational materials on hand? At times, we all have vague expectations for our children—"I'd just like him to leave me alone for 15 minutes and not to get into trouble!" However, most young children with autism and related disabilities have significant limitations in how well they can occupy themselves in a manner that we would find acceptable.

Table 1-4 | Areas of the Home and Common Activities

Area of home/ apartment	Common activities
Kitchen	Preparing food, setting table, eating, cleaning up after a meal, washing dishes, putting dishes away, putting groceries away, sweeping the floor, getting food items from the refrigerator or cupboards, talking on the phone, listening to the radio, watering plants, feeding pets
Living room	Reading books or magazines, sitting and talking to other adults, vacuuming
Dining room	Setting the table, eating meals, cleaning up, dusting or waxing furniture, cleaning floors
Bedroom	Making bed, selecting clothing, sorting clothing, vacuum room, dusting room, reading books, listening to music, feeding fish, watering plant
Bathroom	Filling bathtub, starting shower, bathing, using toilet, brushing teeth, applying deodorant, shaving, cleaning mirror, washing sink and bathtub, cleaning toilet
Rec/TV room	Watching TV, playing DVD, playing music, playing card/board games, dusting and vacuuming, sorting and putting away books, videos, DVDs and CDs
Laundry area	Sorting laundry, loading and running washing machine and dryer, folding laundry, ironing
Garage	Sorting tools, sorting outdoor toys, putting toys away, cleaning car, working on building projects

Kitchen Activities

Let's think about activities in the kitchen. Parents prepare, serve, eat, and clean up meals. Another common adult activity in the kitchen is talking on the telephone. We want to think about how a child can help us with activities as well as consider what the child can do while we are engaged in some important activity and do not want to be interrupted.

What can we expect a five-year-old to do in the kitchen? Many people would simply wait for the child to get older—quite frankly, we don't really expect much of typically developing five-year-olds in helping prepare for dinner! However, we know that children with significant learning needs require more time to learn many different skills. So, if we want the child to be able to help us like a typically developing ten-year-old when he is ten, then we must start far earlier than age ten to teach him to help out. We encourage very young children to start participating in household routines in order to provide ample opportunities for them to learn the required skills.

To help set the table, we can reasonably expect a five-year-old to put out the napkins—at first, maybe simply on the plates; over time, next to the plates; still later, folded and under the fork. Instead of asking the child to handle glassware, we could have him put out small paper cups. In teaching him to place the silverware on the table, we could start with the spoons and use plastic knives if we think that is safer.

Bedroom Activities

Using this area-based approach, let's review what we can expect a child to do in his own bedroom. Usually, we expect children to get undressed and dressed, put away and retrieve clothes, make the bed, play with toys and clean up afterwards, possibly use a computer or audio/video equipment, and go to bed. Here, too, we believe that children with autism should be encouraged to participate in these routines as early as possible, using age appropriate goals.

In general, we advise that you anticipate what you are likely to expect of your child when he is three, five, or even ten years older. Be as specific as you can with particular skills. (See Chapter 5 for examples of how to write a task-analysis for complex skills.) Next, try to determine how much of that skill set your child can currently do. Can he do any of the steps by himself? What type of help does he now need for these skills? Next, think of how you can simplify the task so that it is more age appropriate for your child. For example, you may want to involve fewer steps now than he'll need in three years. You may want to modify the materials involved so that they are more durable, lightweight, or safer to handle, or make similar alterations. It is important to consider the types of communications issues that can arise within each activity as well, and we will take a more detailed look at some of these goals within Chapter 3.

For example, while we may not expect a five-year-old to pick out his clothes and put each item on independently, we would want to teach him to participate as fully as possible in getting and putting on his clothes. Choosing clothes can involve having him follow your instructions regarding what item to wear (e.g., "Pick up your pants" vs. "Pick up your shoes"); details about the item (e.g., "Take the blue shirt" vs. "Take the red shirt"); where to find the clothes (e.g., "Open your dresser" vs. "Open the closet"); and so on.

If your child has difficulties understanding language, you can arrange to teach him the same skills without giving verbal instructions like those we just described. For example, you can set out on his bed his father's biggest sweatshirt, a shirt from a Barbie doll, and his own shirt. There is no need to say, "Take your shirt." You merely need to encourage him with gestures to take a shirt. If he chooses the wrong shirt, simply encourage him to put it on. When that fails, immediately encourage him to pick up his own shirt. It is not necessary to have him immediately take his shirt off and try to choose again. Instead, the next time he needs to choose—most likely the next morning—repeat the choice, and if he chooses correctly, praise him for his cleverness while helping him put on his shirt. At other times, you can offer him choices between huge sneakers, baby doll shoes, and his own sneakers or other similar comparisons.

Prioritizing Goal Setting

Once you have identified a number of skills and behavior problems that you want to address, you will need to prioritize your goals. Clearly, you will not be able to devote concentrated time and effort to everything. You could pick the most difficult problem behaviors to start, but it is likely that these are behaviors that have a long history and may involve many steps to change. We advise focusing first on the skills that would have the most dramatic effect upon your family life if your child acquired them. Teaching your child skills also will involve the use of powerful reinforcers and this will help keep a positive spotlight within your family. (See Chapter 2.) You may want to give added weight to skills that will affect several family members, thus assuring that everyone in the family will have a chance to help promote new skills at home. For example, teaching your child to play quietly with toys or other materials will benefit everyone in your home because then your child can always have something fun to do when others need to do something that does not directly involve him.

How Can We Write Reasonable Goals?

Once you have selected some goals, you will want to write them down so that they are clear to everyone else at home. Try to keep the descriptions relatively simple and straightforward, but at the same time, descriptive of an action. For example, your first impulse may be to write, "Joey will be happy playing" but there will be many different meanings of "happy" within your home. Instead, you could write, "Joey will play with his cars for 10 minutes without help." This type of description is something that everyone can readily agree upon and directly measure. In fact, your aim is to write a description of the goal in such a way that everyone can count or measure the action in the same way.

Here are pairs of potential goals within your home. Please look at each pair and see if you can tell which ones lead to direct measurement and which ones are too vague or indirect:

a. Zach will dress himself quickly.
b. Zach will put on his underwear, socks, pants, shirt, shoes, and belt within 10 minutes of being told to get dressed in the morning.

a. Maria will hit with her fist no more than 2 times per week.
b. Maria will be less aggressive.

a. Phillip will wash his clothes.
b. Phillip will take his laundry basket to the basement, put his clothes in the washing machine, add soap, set the dial correctly, and start the machine within 10 minutes after seeing "laundry time" on his written schedule.

As you can readily see, in each pair, one description is too vague to lead to a direct way to measure or count the action, while the other one is narrow enough to permit two (or more) people to easily agree if the action occurred. Yes, it takes a bit more time to write goals in this detailed fashion, but you will end up avoiding many arguments as to whether or not something important happened.

How Many Lessons at Once?

We think it is a good idea for parents to remember to focus on only one lesson at a time. For example, your goal might be to teach your child to pick out his clothes by listening to your instructions. If so, after he picks his clothes, you should help him quickly put them on rather than starting another lesson on how to put on a shirt. When you want to teach him how to put on a shirt, simply give him the shirt you want him to wear rather than adding another layer (such as choosing the shirt) to the lesson. As your child's skills improve, you can combine tasks, such as having him listen to your instructions as well as putting it on by himself.

We do not mean that children cannot do more than one thing at a time. For example, we can encourage a child to talk about what he is putting on while getting dressed, but it will be most effective to decide ahead of time whether you are focusing your attention on what he is saying or how he is getting dressed. If you are trying to give feedback on both skills, you are likely to confuse your child.

Should We All Do the Same Thing at the Same Time?

Many families enjoy spending time together while in the family room or living room; often, this time is centered around the TV. While some children with autism and related disabilities like to watch particular cartoons or favorite videotapes, they may want to watch the same show too often for everyone else in the family to enjoy. What can they do while their family is watching other shows or videos? Although you may hope that your child will enjoy what you watch, achieving that goal in the near future is probably unlikely. Therefore, you should plan for your child to do something else when other family members are watching a TV program he does not enjoy. If your child needs to learn a new skill in order to do something else, then this is yet another thing to add to your list of skills to teach your child.

One family knew that their daughter enjoyed the sound and music on her favorite movie video, so they bought the CD of the music from the movie and taught her to listen with headphones. They then taught her to sit in the family room listening to her music while everyone else watched TV. At first, this worked for only 5 minutes at a stretch, but over time, they were able to increase that time to about 30 minutes. Another family noticed that their son liked to build complex designs with his Lego® set. They reserved his Lego playtime for when they wanted to watch TV. Then, they would put the blocks out on a table in the room so that they could generally watch what he was doing without having to pay attention to him moment by moment.

To find something your child can do while the family is otherwise occupied, observe what he likes to do independently or start to teach him some quiet but independent activities. Remember, teaching a child to engage in appropriate activities independently for significant periods of time will be a gradual process, requiring great patience from your family. It may take a full year to progress from 2 to 3 minutes of quiet time to 20 to 30 minutes—and your end goal should be tempered by the age of your child. Rarely do 4-year-olds play alone and constructively for 30 minutes or more.

In addition to thinking about how to occupy your child when everyone is gathered in the living room or family room, consider the other areas of your home where you spend significant amounts of time or that you use on a consistent and frequent basis. For example, you may not spend a great deal of time in the laundry area, but doing the wash is something that occurs over and over. Here, too, you can choose between teaching your child to participate with you in some manner or you may want to teach him something to do when you need to spend time here.

How Is a Home Different from a School?

If your child receives special education, a team has worked with you to develop an Individualized Education Program (IEP). In general, these plans are constructed after a specialist has reviewed the skill deficits and strengths your child displayed on some standardized assessment(s). From this list, team members most likely selected certain areas that needed to be addressed and noted them in general terms. For example, a teacher may have suggested that your child needs to work on "attending skills" and on "knowing colors and shapes"; a speech/language pathologist may have proposed goals related to learning receptive and expressive communication skills; another specialist may have suggested that your child needs to improve his sense of balance. From these general descriptions of skills your child needs to learn came more specific descriptions of lesson plans detailing how the staff would teach specific skills. But how can parents best address their child's skill deficits in the home?

Rather than trying to convert your home into a school, we suggest that you examine your home for opportunities to work on the same set of skills that staff are trying to address at school. The routines you've already identified earlier in this chapter will become a great source of teaching opportunities. Below are some examples of how you can look at common routines to find teachable opportunities throughout your home and across the day.

By examining the routines in the laundry area you can find opportunities to work on many of the basic skills your child is taught at school. For example, you can teach your child to sort or match clothes by: a) type (shirt vs. pants), b) size (large, medium, small), c) color tone (lights vs. darks), d) specific colors (red vs. blue), e) specific people (the child's vs. Dad's or Mom's items), or even f) clean versus dirty. When sorting, you begin with a large pile of clothes (possibly in a laundry basket) and teach your child to go through the items, placing the t-shirts in the washing machine but the socks and pants into another basket. When matching, you can place some light clothes in one basket and some dark items in another and guide your child to place the remaining items in the proper baskets. You can add various communication goals within these activities (e.g., instruction following, naming items or attributes, asking for items, etc.), but that is not mandatory. In fact, learning the steps of the routine should be taught before working on these communication goals. (See Chapter 3 for guidance on communication goals.)

It may be difficult for young children to take wet clothes out of the washing machine and put them into the dryer but you can teach an intermediate step, such as having them help place some small items from a basket into the dryer. After the clothes are dry, you can again work on sorting or matching, or you can work on learning how to handle the clean clothes—folding them, putting them into baskets, taking them to the bedroom, and putting them neatly into dressers. You can adjust the degree of assistance at each step (we will describe specific teaching strategies in Chapter 6) according to your child's current skill level. For example, you may complete some of the folding while leaving the last step for your child to complete. Or, you can put two socks next to each other and simply have your child place one atop the other; later, you can add the goal of having your child find the matching sock that you pull out of the pile.

Look at Table 1-5 to compare lessons that may be taught at school but also could be taught at home. As you can see, some of the materials you might use for teaching at home are the same as materials used at school, and some are different.

Table 1-5 | Comparing Lessons at School and Home

School Lesson	Home Activity	Home Materials
Expressive Labeling	Name common areas, items, activities	Pets, toys, clothes, cutlery, TV, bed, table, foods
Receptive Identification	Get or point to common items; put object with common items	Pets, toys, clothes, cutlery, TV, bed, table, foods
Direction Following	"put ____ on ____" "Give it to ____"	Hug a toy or pet; shake hands or kiss people; push or put away a toy car; scribble with or pick up a crayon
Sorting	Separating items into groups	Cans on one shelf/bottles on another; dolls in one box/toy cars in another; socks in one drawer/shirts in another; pots in one cabinet/paper bags in another
Matching to Sample	Putting similar items together	Laundry: put clothes in piles by family member, size, color, type, etc. Kitchen: put like utensils, dishes, cups, pots, etc. together

Review

The first element of the Pyramid Approach involves issues related to the functional activities we want our children to develop over time. Functional activities include skills that will serve the individual throughout his lifetime and lead to greater independence in different settings. In order to help your child develop skills that will last a lifetime both in and around a home, you will need to create lessons that are practical and that function in these settings.

To determine what is important to teach, consider your child's skill deficits as well as the problematic behaviors that lead to stress within the family. Review your routines both by the time of day and the location within your home where activities occur. Be prepared to spend several years to help your child acquire skills that will lead to greater independence. In part, this goal can be accomplished by considering how your child can participate in many activities and routines throughout the day and within all areas of your home. We will continue moving through the elements of the Pyramid Approach in the following chapters. We next focus our attention on how to motivate your child to learn these new skills before we address how to teach them step-by-step.

2 Using Motivational Strategies to Build Successful Change

Donna Martin loves to ride in the family car. She likes to go to fast-food restaurants but she does not like going to the mall. Her parents usually first take Donna to get a quick meal before going to the mall. Still, every time they park the car in the mall, Donna launches into a routine litany of complaints about how much she dislikes the mall and her behavior escalates until her parents take her out of the mall. Donna's parents have set a goal for their daughter to tolerate trips to the mall. However, they feel at a loss as to how to motivate Donna to enjoy going with them to the mall and other places in the community.

Like many parents, the Martins have tried many ways to motivate their child to do things she isn't eager to do. Most of their attempts have been fruitless. One unsuccessful strategy that parents frequently try is appeasing the child by buying anything she wants. Of course, on the next visit to that same store, the child will expect to receive whatever treat was purchased the last time. Another common approach is to temporarily remove the child from the store, wait for her to calm down, and then reenter the store. But here, the child learns that a tantrum may lead to leaving or momentarily escaping from the store, which may be precisely what she wants. And when she reenters the store, there often are treats to help persuade her to stay calm.

Clearly, it's one thing for parents to set a goal for their child to achieve, and another thing to help the child achieve that goal without inadvertently teaching her something unintended. When children are very young, we are used to helping them perform many tasks that we hope they will complete independently as they grow older. However, for some children the problem of motivation remains acute for some time. For example, if a child's parents have always tied her shoes, when they now expect her to do so on her own, she may be thinking, "Why should I do this myself? You've always done such a fine job of tying my shoes!" The key to getting your child to learn your lesson is to ensure that she is motivated to achieve that goal.

Reinforcers

How do we best motivate children to learn new skills? Everyone has observed coaches cajoling their players to "try harder" or urging them on by shouts and yells. However, the most important leader in the field of behavior analysis, B.F. Skinner, pointed out that learning is best achieved by the thoughtful use of certain consequences for particular skills. We call those outcomes reinforcers—and they are a teacher's best friends!

Formally, reinforcers are consequences that result in an increased likelihood of the same behavior occurring in similar situations. We often think of reinforcers as rewards, but we need to keep in mind that reinforcers are highly personalized. What works as a reinforcer for one child's behavior may not be effective for another's behavior.

There are two types of changes that might result in a reinforcing outcome:

1. positive reinforcers,
2. negative reinforcers.

Positive Reinforcers. Positive reinforcers are things or events that we introduce or add (and hence are considered "positive") into a situation. For example, you might praise your child for cleaning up the table and find she is more likely to do it again. Or you might give your child time to watch a TV show, read a story, or go outside to fly a kite together with you, or give her a cookie after she demonstrates a skill you are teaching her. Each of these might lead to improved learning.

Negative Reinforcers. Other reinforcers are effective because they take something out of the situation. We call these negative (as in "take away") reinforcers. For example, your child might put on a headset to cope with a noisy mall—reducing the level of noise acts as a reinforcer for wearing the headset. Or your daughter might scream when you tell her to clean her room and you then decide to back off and "not push the issue"—then, after you stop nagging, she completes the task.

Keep It Positive. We advise that you work hard to create as many positive reinforcers as possible and use them frequently when teaching your child skills in and around the house. The frequent use of negative reinforcers is often associated with nagging and threatening. We prefer for you to aim for the development of new skills through positive approaches.

You may have observed your child working on a formal lesson at school (or within an in-home ABA program) and noticed that teachers provided some type of reinforcer following virtually every correct action by your child. At home and in the community, your aim will be to design reinforcement systems that permit you to take advantage of the more natural environment available. We will describe several ways of using powerful reinforcement systems within your home and while you are in your neighborhood. For more information about using reinforcement strategies, including how to figure out which reinforcers are most effective for your child, please read *Incentives for Change,* by Lara Delmolino and Sandra Harris (Woodbine House, 2005).

Taking Advantage of Natural Rewards

Whenever you are considering beginning a lesson, you should first try to identify reinforcers that are natural to the situation. Natural reinforcers are those that are commonly associated with successfully completing some activity. For example, a natural reinforcer to putting on sneakers is being able to run around outside; putting a CD into the CD player leads to the opportunity to listen to music; setting the table leads to eating a meal. In each of these cases, the reward for the task comes immediately upon completion.

Let's consider a number of common activities in and around the home and think about their potential for being associated with naturally occurring rewards. See what rewards you can think about for the end of the list and then try to add some activities and their natural rewards for your child and situation.

Table 2-1 | Areas, Activities, and Related Rewards

Area	Activity	Natural Reward
Kitchen	Cook	Eat
Family Room	Turn on TV	Watch show/videos
Bathroom	Take a bath	Warm (not cold or hot water)
Library	Take out a book	Read on a bench outside
Playground	Climb the slide	Slide down
Grandma's house	Give Grandma a kiss	Smiles and hugs
The Mall	Walking calmly to store	*Your thought?*

What Do We Do When We Can't Find a Natural Reinforcer?

While we believe that natural rewards are best to use, they are not always motivating for children. For example, the primary benefits for brushing teeth are associated with long-term improvements in dental health and a lower risk for dental problems. The benefit of putting the open milk carton in the refrigerator is associated with less spoilage (better taste) over time. These consequences only occur far in the future and thus may be ineffective in motivating young children to brush their teeth or put food away. Toothpaste producers are aware of this problem and try to make

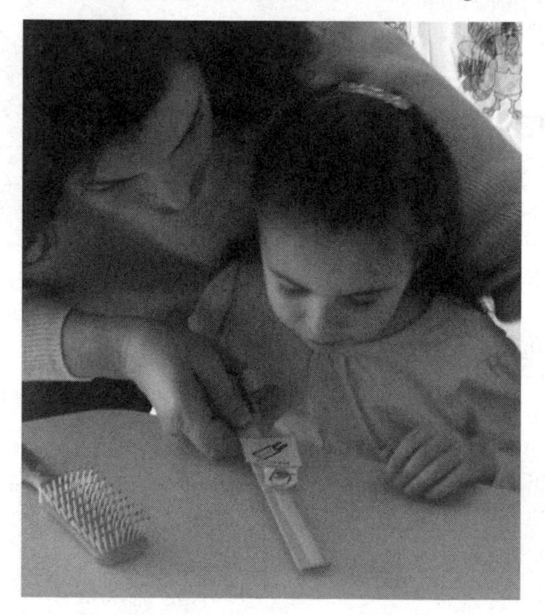

their products taste as pleasing as possible. We also may try to make a special arrangement to bolster the immediate consequences, as when we say, "When you're done brushing your teeth, I'll read your favorite book to you!"

So, whenever possible, try to arrange for natural outcomes, but if you think these are too removed in time from the activity, then be certain to arrange for something rewarding to immediately follow your child's completion of the activity. In either case, we will describe a "reinforcer first" strategy to help your child focus on the natural or arbitrary reward that she can earn by completing the task at hand.

Here is a list of some activities for which "natural" reinforcers may be difficult to identify or difficult to bring to bear immediately. Once again, we hope you'll fill in the blanks and also add some others pertinent to your child:

Table 2-2 | Area, Activity, and Arbitrary Rewards

Area	Activity	Arbitrary Reward
Kitchen	Put silverware away	Watch TV
Family room	Shut off the VCR	Dad reads a book aloud
Bathroom	Use a towel to dry hands	Play alone in bathroom
Library	Walk and look quietly	Points toward earning a book to take out
Playground	Takes turns on the slide	Praise and another chance on the slide
Grandma's house	Sit at the table	*Your thought?*

How and When Do We Make Our Child Aware of the Reinforcer?

As we noted, reinforcers are consequences for certain actions, so perhaps you think you should wait until you observe your child doing that behavior before you introduce the reinforcer. It also may seem natural to start lessons with your instructions or demands. However, we ask you to think about what happened when you went to interview for a new job. Did you agree to start the job without knowing what your salary and benefits would be? In all likelihood, you knew exactly what your reinforcer would be—your salary—for doing the job well before you started to work. We believe we should interact with our children in the same manner that we expect to be treated. We refer to knowing your potential reinforcer before you start the lesson (or job!) as the "reinforcer first strategy."

For example, let's say that Phil hates going to the grocery store and whines persistently whenever his parents make him go. Let's further say that Phil's parents know that he likes to eat bananas. They take him to the supermarket, and tell him (or show him) that they are going to get a banana. They take him directly to the bananas and pick one out. They then go to the checkout line (hopefully it is empty), buy the banana, and allow Phil to immediately eat the banana. Then they go home! This trip was not intended to complete the family's shopping needs. It was only done to help teach Phil that he can go to a store and get something that he likes. Sometime soon, the parents return to the supermarket, again letting Phil know (via their spoken words or with visual cues) that they will buy a banana. This time, while they are walking to the bananas, Mom picks up a box of pasta before picking out the banana. They take both items to checkout, and allow Phil to eat the banana just after they leave the store.

Table 2-3 | Gradually Increasing Skills and Goals in the Community

Visit#	What to buy	Other skills to teach
1	Banana	Walk with Mom and Dad
2	Pasta, banana	Walk with Mom and Dad
3	Pasta, milk, banana	Walk with Mom and Dad Stand at checkout line
4	Pasta, milk, cereal, banana	Walk with Mom and Dad Choose cereal Stand at checkout line
5	Pasta, milk, cereal, cheese, banana	Walk with Mom and Dad Choose cereal Put cereal and cheese on checkout belt Stand at checkout line

Over the next several trips, Phil's family gradually adds more items to the cart before heading to pick up the banana. They also encourage Phil to select other items that he likes to buy. Furthermore, they prompt him to help with some of the items—putting them into the shopping cart, putting items onto the checkout counter, giving the salesperson some money, etc. Notice that each trip starts by reminding Phil about what he will get when he completes the shopping, consistent with our reinforcer first strategy.

At home, it is helpful to avoid beginning interactions with a demand. For example, do not say to your child, "Go clean up your room and then we'll play a game" or "Put the ball away and let's go inside and then we'll look for a movie that we can put into the video machine." By starting with the task, you alert the child to the work to be done. You also may be signaling the end of whatever enjoyable activity the child is currently doing. If you try starting this way, you may not even get to finish your sentence! The demand may immediately lead your child to protest what she has lost or is about to give up. Rather, start with, "Hey, let's play a game! Oh, by the way, we need to clean up first," or, "Want to watch a video? Great! Let's put the ball away and go inside," or, "Let's get a book! Remember, we have to walk quietly to the shelf." In each case, we began by telling the child what the point, or goal, of the activity will be and then said how to get that goal.

If your child does not understand what you are saying, you can show her (via the object or a picture, depending on her level of understanding) what she can earn before you visually indicate what task she will need to complete.

Let's Make a Deal

There may be times when you feel hard pressed to come up with the right deal at the very instant you want your child to do something. In these situations, you may want to remember why you go to work, even at times when you simply aren't thrilled with the idea of working! That's right—we tell ourselves that if we do our work, we will earn a paycheck and then we can use the money for something we want later. That is, we use money in situations where we can't or simply don't want to specify exactly what we are trying to achieve by completing the job. When we earn money, we can choose what we want when we have a chance to spend the money. For some children, earning money—via household chores and other responsibilities—is commonplace. But it only works when the child understands the value of money. If your child does not yet understand money, it won't help to simply give her some when she does a job well. First, children have to learn to appreciate money by learning why it is useful—to buy things. So, before you use money to help motivate your child, you must arrange for her to want to have money.

If you are uncomfortable with using real money at home or in the community, you may want to use some type of point or token system. However, just as with money, you must first teach your child the value of the points or tokens before you try to use them to motivate her.

Teaching the Value of Tokens

To teach the value of the point or token (or real money), start with a simple activity—one that your child can already accomplish. At this stage, the goal is to teach your child that you are trustworthy. When you make a deal, you will hold up your end of the bargain. Let's assume your child can sort the forks from the spoons. Have several of each with you. Before showing them to your child, find out—either by asking or having your child choose directly—what she would like at the moment. It may help to offer her a limited range of choices rather than risk her requesting something you do not have available at the moment or something that is currently impractical. Whether you present these choices verbally or visually will depend upon your child's skill level.

You may want to use a simple visual aid such as the one in Figure 1 or one of your own design. The key elements will include information about what is to be earned, how much work needs to be done or how long the job will last, and some way of monitoring progress toward the goal. You can use pieces of a puzzle (as in Figure 2) or, for some children, simply have them earn a letter toward spelling out the name of what they want to earn.

Once the child selects what she wants (remember, reinforcer first!) put some type of visual symbol representing her chosen reward on the "work" card that has one open circle on it (or one place for the puzzle piece, etc.). Then have her do something very simple and very quick, such as put one fork in one container and one spoon in another. Immediately give her a token while you praise her hard work. Have her

Figure 1: Token-type reinforcement system

put the token on the open circle. Since there is only one open circle, she has now completed the deal! Have her cash out by giving you the token that's on the card and immediately give her whatever she was working for. She does not have to ask for that item again because she already indicated what she wanted (but don't stop her if she does ask on her own). Practice earning and redeeming tokens with this and other simple tasks until she independently gives you the token when it is placed on the card. You also can add a small amount of work required to earn that single token. At that point, your child will have shown you that she understands that the token leads to the reward.

Figure 2: Puzzle-type reinforcement system

You then can stretch the deal by placing two open circles on the card. You can stretch this two-circle deal by having her do somewhat more work for the first token but slightly less work for the second. When she seems to catch on to the fact that she can cash out when both circles are full, then you can gradually add a third, fourth, and fifth circle (see Figure 3 for an example). We often stop when we have reached five circles and continue to stretch how much work the child needs to do for each token rather than keep on adding circles, although for some children, adding circles will work just fine. For example, if you are using the system to help your child clean up her toys, at first you may want to give her a token after each toy is put away. However, by the time you are using several tokens, you can wait until she puts two or three toys away before giving her the next token. While you want to gradually increase how much "work" she will do for each token, do not make the demand so high per token that she quits!

In general, we do not recommend taking a child's tokens away once she has earned them. When managing some behaviors, however, it may be useful to start out with a number of tokens and then gradually remove them. See the section on "Fines" in Chapter 7 for information on this strategy.

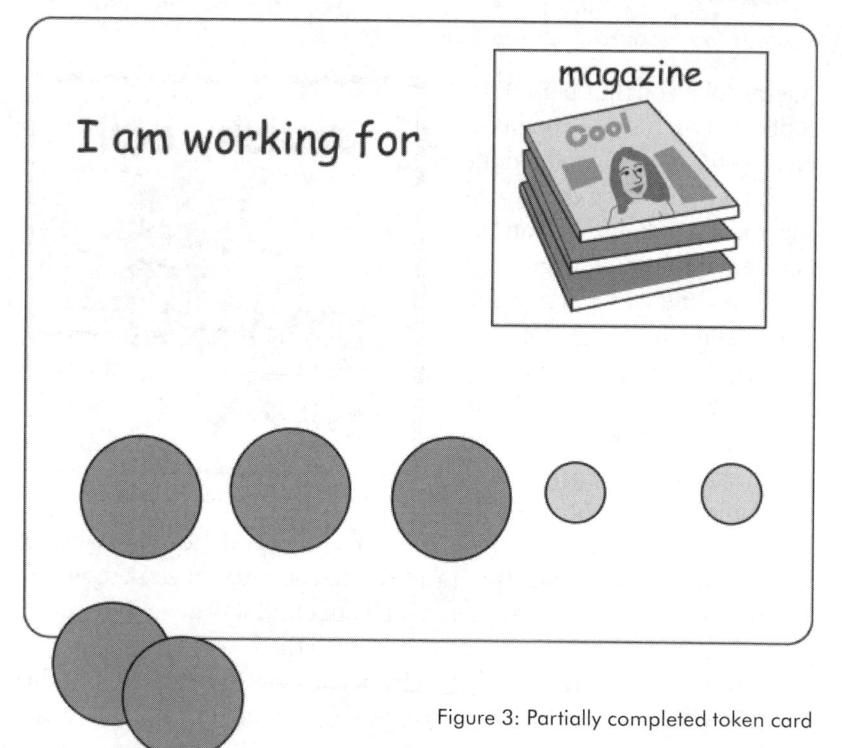

Figure 3: Partially completed token card

Remember, we are not saying that you should use money or tokens all the time. In fact, you may only need to use them infrequently at home or in the neighborhood because there should be an abundance of natural rewards available. But if you teach your child to use tokens properly, they can provide powerful and consistent systems to motivate her in situations where it may be difficult or impractical to find an immediate reward. You can take work cards and tokens with you when you go out of the house in case you need to set up some quick deals while visiting neighbors, playing in the park, or shopping. Also, these systems can act as a type of clock for the child who cannot tell time. For example, rather than telling her she will be able to watch TV in 10 minutes, you may be able to set up a deal in which she can turn on the TV after she has earned 5 tokens. Then, all you do is arrange for a simple activity for her and pace handing out the tokens so that you give her the last one after about 10 minutes.

Catch 'Em Being Good!

Everyone agrees that it is a good idea to catch our children being good— the hard part is doing it often enough! Several factors make this good advice tough to follow. For one thing, who decides what's "enough?" Well, we should gauge this on our children, since it is their needs that we are trying to meet. And what does "being good" mean? Sometimes, it is simply a matter of not getting into trouble! Think about times when you've been busy with something— balancing your checkbook, cooking a meal, or just sitting and relaxing a bit. While you're doing that, your child is quietly playing or doing something nondestructive and nondemanding. Most of us would sit there as long as we can, enjoying the quiet opportunity to do what we want to do. If you think about it, you'll realize that eventually your child is likely to do something that forces you to pay attention. She may scream, knock something over, break something, etc. At that point you are forced to pay attention and stop what you are doing. In the long run, it would have been more helpful to pay attention to your child while she was doing something positive or at least nondemanding.

Sometimes we adults may need some help to remember to do things that will benefit our children in the long run while involving some effort in the here and now. What are some options to help us remember to reinforce our children for good behavior?

In school situations, we have advised teachers to use tape recordings (or CDs, if that's the technology you use) that play a nonirritating tone on a planned basis. We call these Audio Reinforcement Reminder Tones. For example, a tape may be set to play a tone, on average, every one to five minutes. When the teachers hear the tone, their job is to catch some student doing something positive as quickly as possible. We have found that rates of praise rise dramatically while these tones are in use and are sustained over long periods of time. Furthermore, without any direct suggestions, the number of negative or corrective comments from these same teachers noticeably drops. Some families who have observed this positive classroom atmosphere like it so much that they use a similar system during their most chaotic times at home—those times when it is easy to forget about their quiet child. Other parents have found this strategy somewhat out of place within their home.

An alternative to using reminder tones at home is to use a token system and set a goal of handing out a set number of tokens for positive behavior every hour. For example, put 10 tokens in your pocket with the goal of having none left in an hour's time. Carrying around the tokens helps to remind you to give them out.

You may have some other way to cue yourself, but we promise it's not easy to remember when you are very busy with your own activities unless you plan to give yourself a helpful reminder. For instance, you might cut up a picture of your child's favorite fast food meal and hand out pieces of the puzzle throughout the afternoon, ending up at the restaurant when the completed puzzle is exchanged for the real deal!

Better Work—Better Pay!

Sometimes, parents ask us what to do when their child tries something but doesn't do it very well. Perhaps your child has cleaned up her room but has left several toys on the floor. Perhaps she set the dinner table for four instead of five. Perhaps your child asked for something but you expected a polite "please" that was omitted. Or, perhaps you know you have to help your child while she is still learning a skill but she certainly has tried hard to perform the task. How can you encourage your child to continue trying while letting her know that improvement is still warranted?

When people compete during a track meet (or some other related competition), the top three racers may all win ribbons, though only one wins the race. In some sense, we can look at the different ways that a child performs a task as several actions competing with each other. Some attempts should earn ribbons even if they aren't the best, while others may not earn anything distinct other than, "good try." For example, if your child sets the table for all five family members, she will certainly earn high praise and some time to watch a favorite TV show. However, if she sets the table for four, rather than five, you could praise her, then follow up with some assistance to help her complete the job, and then give her access to either some less-preferred activity or a shorter time to watch TV. In contrast, if your child just puts one spoon on the table, you might make a short, positive comment about starting the task, then provide lots of assistance to complete the task, and finally give her some modest reward. In other words, if putting one spoon earned the same outcome as completing setting the table for five, why would anyone work harder to complete the job independently?

Our general rule is to reinforce all appropriate behaviors but to reserve our big rewards for the best performances. If we need to help our children, then their reward should not be as powerful as when they complete the task independently. The procedure of rewarding different levels of independence with different size rewards is described as using *differential reinforcement*. This strategy will encourage persistence while also promoting greater independence in your child.

Is Everything a Lesson?

In this book, we describe many ways that parents, other family members, and professionals can teach various skills to children with autism and related disabilities within their own homes and neighborhoods. While reading this book, you may feel that we want you to spend every waking moment creating and implementing lessons! That's not our goal! First, we hope that you will encourage your child to participate in independent recreational or leisure activities—ones that you will not have to closely supervise or participate in.

Furthermore, there are many activities in and around the home that do not involve lessons. For example, your child must take a certain medicine at a set time. While you would like your child to cooperate, your parental responsibilities demand that you assure that the medicine is taken at the prescribed time. Or, you hear one of the house fire-alarms blasting and it may well signal a real fire. No one would expect your child to follow a 22-step task-analysis and put on her coat independently—your sole goal is to get the child out of the house safely! In this situation, there is no lesson to be taught regarding putting on a coat.

How do we distinguish between times we teach as opposed to times we take care of our children? In part, this depends on how much active participation we expect from the child and whether the degree of participation will alter the outcome. In the examples from the last paragraph, parents assure the outcome—taking the medicine and getting safely out of the house—regardless of how much or how little the child participated. On the other hand, you may be teaching your child a skill, such as making toast. While you'd like her to learn to do it on her own, for now, even if she simply takes the bread you hand her and allows you to guide her to put the bread into the toaster, you will still give her the toast when it's ready. As her skills improve, you may decide that she needs to complete more of the task independently. So, unless she helps push down the toaster-arm, you let her eat cold bread rather than warm toast. That is, you decide to use differential reinforcement to encourage greater independence. This strategy implies that you are teaching a lesson and not just feeding your child.

Whenever you decide that you are teaching rather than taking care of your child, then you must consider your child's motivation to complete the chore that you believe she should complete. As we noted earlier, we support the general strategy of making deals in such situations. That is, make sure your child knows ahead of time what she will earn or receive for completing the lesson.

What Is the Ultimate Goal for Using Reinforcers?

As we have noted, it is important to gradually reduce how often you reinforce your child's appropriate actions so that you see more and more action for fewer and fewer reinforcers over time. But will we ever totally eliminate reinforcers? This question can lead to interesting philosophical debates! But at a practical level it may be best to expect that reinforcement will most likely continue at some level, although it may become quite rare.

Think for a moment about how you learned to read. When you were very young, your teacher most likely reinforced very small actions—naming letters and saying their sounds. Then, the teacher changed the deal so that you needed to read individual words before she reinforced you, and then you needed to read short phrases. Gradually, you needed to read longer and longer sentences, then paragraphs and chapters, and finally entire books. Over time, the number of times that you received direct reinforcement for reading books greatly diminished. But has reinforcement disappeared entirely? Most likely, you still read books and occasionally you talk about enjoying (or hating!) a particular book—the conversation you have about the book is a type of reinforcer for reading the book. In addition, you sometimes read something that provides information that helps you solve a problem or provides insight that helps you address an important issue more effectively—each of these outcomes is likely a reinforcer for reading. Although a teacher is no longer dispensing reinforcers for your reading, the natural community provides for this arrangement. So too, many of the skills you teach your child will eventually be reinforced by society at large and you will no longer have to make explicit plans to reinforce all skills.

Review

In this chapter, we have reviewed the next element of the Pyramid Approach by focusing on motivational factors. Properly motivating your child to learn important skills in the home and community is crucial if she is going to achieve independence. We have emphasized the use of powerful reinforcement systems that accentuate the use of positive reinforcers. Our first choice within any lesson is to try to use reinforcers that seem natural to the circumstances. However, that may not always be practical. In these situations, we need to develop systematic reinforcement systems that help remind our children about the reinforcers available for doing many different skills. Gradually reducing the frequency of reinforcement is another important goal that parents can achieve both within and around the home. The next area of the Pyramid Approach involves social and communication skills, areas that are crucial for children to fully participate in our society.

3 Important Communication Goals in and around the Home

Shelby's parents are reading in the family room. Shelby comes in and walks up to the bookcase. She reaches for a book on the top shelf and when she can't quite reach it, she drags a chair over to the shelves, climbs on the chair, and gets the book. Her parents certainly know what she wants.

Did Shelby communicate?

Josh is playing in the sandbox while his father is sitting on a nearby park bench. Josh leaves the sandbox, walks over to his father, looks at his father's eyes while he pulls him to the seesaw, sits his father on one end, and runs to sit on the other end. His father immediately pushes him up and down and Josh laughs out loud.

Did Josh communicate?

Hunter is playing in the family room in front of a big window. Suddenly the trash truck pulls up in front of his house. It is very big and very noisy. Hunter, who is about 15 months old, stops, gasps, and looks at his mother. As she turns to him, he looks back at the truck, points to it, and looks back at Mom. He continues looking back and forth between his mother and the truck until she, too, sees the truck and reacts: "Wow! That's a loud truck!" Hunter has not yet developed any whole words to say, but his mother certainly understands that he wants her to react.

Did Hunter communicate?

What Is Communication?

Let's consider the first scenario. Shelby directed her behavior to the shelf, chair, and then the book. Actions that are directed to the environment and that lead to rewarding outcomes are not communicative! Even though her parents were sitting nearby, Shelby did not interact with them in any way, so we conclude that she did not communicate. In fact, her behavior would have been exactly the same had they not been in the room. Shelby's parents, by watching her, could have *interpreted* that she wanted the book, but that interpretation does not mean that Shelby communicated with them. Their presence had no impact upon her actions.

In each of the next two scenarios, the children did something directed to their parents, who responded in some way. Josh's dad pushed him on the seesaw, while Hunter's mom reacted to the truck he was pointing out. Even though these children did not say words, everyone recognizes that they did communicate with their parents.

So, communication involves at least two people. One person (we will call this person "the *speaker,*" even when no speech is involved) directs a behavior of some sort to another person (we will call this person "the *listener,*" even when speech is not involved). The listener then reacts to the speaker in a manner that is rewarding to the speaker. In the last scenario above, Hunter looks at his mother and then back to the truck. He does this again and again until his mother notices the truck and makes some comment about it. He definitely communicated! The message he delivered did not involve spoken words; he gasped and directed his mother's eyes to the truck by looking from her to the truck. Likewise, while Josh did not say anything, his actions involving his father lead his father to begin playing with him on the seesaw!

Understanding the basics of communication will help parents better cope with situations in which communication has broken down. The root of many behavior management problems lies in either the lack of communication or miscommunication. While it is beyond the scope of this book to review many effective strategies to teach functional communication, it will be helpful to review some of the fundamental issues associated with communication.

Why Children Communicate

Before we make plans to teach communication in the home and community, it is helpful to look at the conditions that might affect a child's communication. Sometimes children are chatty and simply want to spend time interacting with others. Sometimes children need or want a specific item from someone. Some children are great at starting interactions and other children tend to wait for someone else to start a conversation. Therefore, we need to look at *why* children communicate, and under *what* circumstances, or when children communicate.

In 1957, B.F. Skinner published a highly influential book, *Verbal Behavior,* in which he offered an analysis of language from a behavior analytic perspective. His book has led to many studies that have supported many of his interpretations as well as to the development of particular intervention strategies. For example, the PECS (Picture Exchange Communication System) protocol was developed based upon the principles laid out by Skinner. In his book, Skinner proposed a number of terms to help clarify specific types of communicative acts, and we encourage readers to learn more about his ideas. Within this chapter we will use colloquial terms but attempt to highlight the function connected with different types of language use.

Let's look at the situation in which Josh directed his actions toward his father until his father pushed him on the seesaw. The outcome—playing on the seesaw—was specifically what Josh wanted. We call this type of communication a *request* (in Skinner's analysis, this is a "mand"). The *direct* outcome for Josh was something material or concrete that he wanted.

There is another type of outcome or reward for communication. Think about Hunter and the interaction with his mother. Hunter noticed the big truck and got his mother to notice it too. He didn't expect or want his mother to get the truck for him. He wanted his mother's attention and for her to see what he saw. He wanted something social from his mother—her attention, her praise, her apparent enjoyment of her conversation with him. He did not get anything material from his communication, such as playing on the seesaw as Josh received. Instead, he *commented* to his mother, who provided him with a *social* reaction (a "tact" in Skinner's terminology).

We can divide the main purposes (or functions) of communication into requests and comments. When we want to teach communication, our first job will be to consider what purpose a communicative act will serve for the child. Furthermore, what we know about the child may influence our lesson goals. For example, we know that social rewards for very young children with autism and related disabilities tend not to be very effective. Therefore, it may be difficult to start communication lessons with very young children with autism by targeting communication skills that primarily serve a commenting function, such as simply naming common objects. It is likely to be more useful to the child to begin teaching him how to *request* their most important reinforcers.

When Children Communicate

In addition to looking at the "why" or the consequences of communicating, we also must look at the conditions that exist prior to communication. These conditions, known as *antecedents,* will affect how we plan our communication lessons. For example, Will, Julie, and Mike can say the word "swing." Today when Will's dad takes him to the neighborhood park, as soon as Will sees the swing, he grabs his dad's arm, says, "Swing!" and pulls Dad toward the swings. When Julie and her dad arrive at the park, Julie stands at the edge of the playground. Her dad waits for Julie to let him know what she wants to do first, but Julie doesn't say anything. Dad asks, "What do you want to do?" and Julie then says, "Swing." When Mike arrives with his mom, she too waits to see if he will tell her what he wants to do. When he doesn't, she says, "What do you want to do?" When Mike still doesn't respond, she says, "Can you say 'Swing'?" Mikes says "Swing." Soon all three children are happily being pushed on the swing.

Although all three children said "swing," and all three children got to go on the swing, each child actually did something different. Will saw the swing and *initiated* a request for the swing. Julia did not initiate, but she *responded* to her dad's question about what she wanted to do. Mike did not initiate or respond to his mom's direct questions, but he did *imitate* her by saying, "swing." Thus, although each child said "swing," one child initiated, one child responded to a prompt or cue, and one child imitated a model—three distinct behaviors.

It would be fantastic if children could automatically interchange these behaviors with each other. That is, if we teach one form, the child can immediately use the other two. Unfortunately, our knowledge of typical language development and the general principles of learning have taught us that such is not the case. Each of these types of communication skills initially develops independently. At some point in their development (usually when their communication repertoire grows to a reasonable size) children eventually can generalize (or transfer) new vocabulary across each type of communication skill. However, when we begin to teach children with communication deficits, we will have to teach each of these communication skills independently. So, we must decide which skill to teach first. We recommend teaching initiation first, as this enables children to be independent communicators.

Children as "Listeners"

We said that communication involves two people, a speaker and a listener. So far we have discussed teaching children to be the speaker. In addition to learning to use communication, children also must learn to understand communication directed to them. Children learn to be the speaker because of the social or tangible outcomes associated with interacting with someone else. Children learn to be the listener for the same two outcomes. Some directions that we give our children involve natural outcomes that they enjoy. For example, if Dad says, "Go get your ball," the outcome for his daughter doing what he said is getting to play ball with Dad.

Sometimes we give directions because they help *us* in some way. Mom may be thirsty and say to her son, "Please bring me a Coke." Mom can only get her drink if her son understands what she said. But what does her son get out of the interaction? Hopefully, Mom will politely thank him for getting her drink. Remember that not all children with disabilities find polite praise highly motivating. For these children, teaching them to follow directions that are personally useful is more likely to be successful than teaching them to follow directions that primarily benefit other people.

There will also be times when you will need to give instructions to your child for his own safety or "just because I said so!" In essence, these types of demands should result in compliance. As children get older, they may find themselves in such situations more frequently, such as when they need to listen to what the boss tells them at work simply because she is the boss. In our perspective, compliance is something that we build in over time and is rarely the first type of instructional situation we want to design. That is, we suggest working on:

1. instructions that initially lead to natural and powerful rewards that directly benefit the child, and then on
2. instructions for which the social rewards are clear, and, hopefully, effective as well.
3. Finally, we will need to work on instructions for which immediate reinforcement may be lacking.

For example, if your child has never listened to what you say, you would obviously not start teaching him to listen on a busy street corner and try to get your child to obey when you say, "stop!" Instead, you would develop good listening skills in safe situations before carefully applying them in potentially more dangerous settings.

Summary of the Reasons Children Communicate

Think of all the "whys" and "whens" associated with the word "video." In the role of the speaker, your son might imitate the word, answer a question (e.g., "What do you want? or "What's that?") with the word, or initiate with the word. In all three conditions he could either get a video (requesting) or he might receive some social praise (commenting). In the role of the listener, he might follow a direction involving the word "video" that results in getting to watch a video or a warm "thank you!" from you. Look at the flowchart on the next page and you'll note *eight different* skills associated with communicating the word, "video!"

Are There Many Ways to Communicate?

Are there times when we speak but do not communicate? Remember, communicative acts must be directed toward another person. Does your daughter ever sing a song or recite dialogue from a video when she is alone? Do you ever sing in the shower or while driving alone?

Flowchart 3-1 | Communication Associations with Single Words

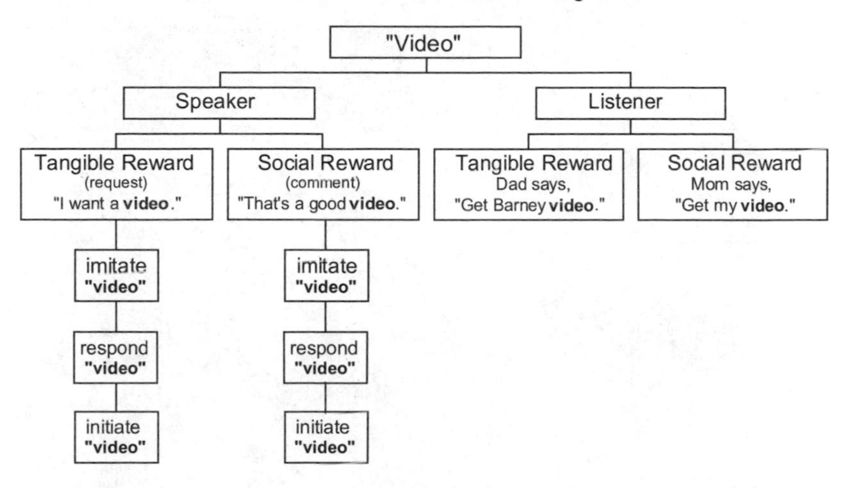

Such talking and singing would not meet our definition of communication because the speaker or singer is not directing his or her words or song to a "listener" or communicative partner. In fact, many of us quit singing when we are joined by another person!

Some children with autism and related disabilities repeat words, phrases, jingles from TV or the radio, or entire dialogs from movies without understanding what they are saying. They are not constructing the sentences from words they know how to use but, rather, are repeating the sounds for reasons not related to communication. Therefore, when we assess a child's ability to communicate, we must go beyond a simple description of what words the child can say.

Is speaking the only way we communicate? Of course not! We also use gestures or "body language." Some people use sign language with others who understand sign language. Sometimes we write notes to ourselves or to others. You might jot down a "to do" list for yourself or leave your kids a note to read. Sometimes we use or respond to pictures. For example, you might save a picture of a particular object you've been wanting and show it to your partner a few weeks before your birthday!

Each of these examples involves a different type of communication modality—using our hands and other parts of our body, using print or pictures, etc. Each type of communication—including speech—has its advantages and disadvantages. Competent communication is possible through several different types of modalities. Even when we can

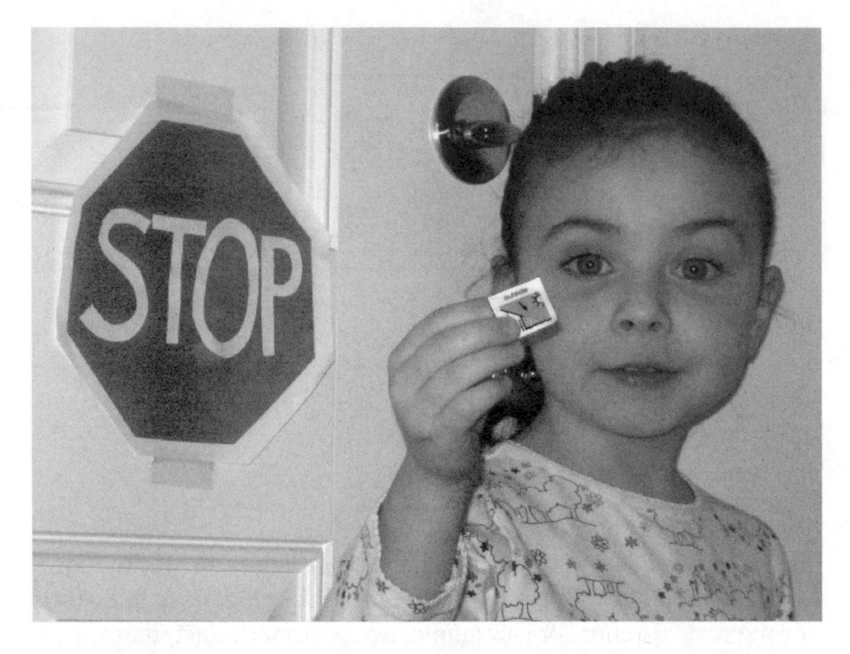

speak, we often combine several modalities when communicating. Some of us use expansive hand and arm movements and exaggerated facial expressions to emphasize certain points.

If your child does not yet speak or doesn't speak in a manner others understand, he might be using some form of *augmentative or alternative communication (AAC).* He could use an electronic device with a synthesized or recorded voice. He might use pictures within the Picture Exchange Communication System (PECS). He might use sign language or type and print messages for others to read. If a professional such as a teacher or speech-language pathologist has recommended that your child use some form of AAC, this doesn't mean that the teacher or SLP are "giving up" on speech. What it means is that the goal is to provide your child with a means to effectively communicate right now, while speech production and development are being addressed. Will these alternative modalities "inhibit" speech development? We know from many years of research that the answer is "NO!!" Use of AAC systems will not inhibit or prevent the development of speech. In fact, many researchers report that these systems actually enhance speech development (Glennen, 1997; Mirenda, 2002). To learn more about these visual modes of communication, a good introduction is *A Picture's Worth: PECS and Other Visual*

Communication Strategies in Autism, by Andy Bondy and Lori Frost (Woodbine House, 2002).

Modalities for "Listening"

Just as there are several modalities our children can use to communicate with us, there also are different modalities we may use that they will need to understand. For example, you may be on the other side of the playground from your child and he may be unlikely to hear what you are saying. In this case, you might wave your arms to gesture for him to come over to you. Will he understand what your arm motions mean? Similarly, there will be times when you point to critical things or places in your home or community and you will want your child to be able to understand your gestures.

There are many types of visual signals in our society. Some of these involve printed words. That is one reason we put so much emphasis in school on teaching children to read. But even if a child cannot read, he still will benefit from understanding different visual cues in the environment. For example, while some bathrooms in your community are labeled with the words "men" or "women," think of how many different pictures/drawings are on the doors! We once counted over 25 different ways of indicating gender for bathrooms within a 10-mile radius of a school in Delaware. Many of us understand a stop sign by its shape and color long before we can see the word printed in the middle. Therefore, it is important to teach children to respond to visual cues because they are so common out in your neighborhood.

Setting Goals for Critical Communication

To meet our goal for children to grow up to live and work as independently as possible, they must learn certain communication skills. These skills are critical because, if your child cannot calmly and effectively engage in each skill, then he or she will most likely try other means to obtain the same outcome. Typically, we are not thrilled with these other "means"—crying, fussing, shouting, hitting, etc. We have identified nine such skills, some of which are skills to be used as a speaker and some to be used as a listener. See Table 3-1.

Table 3-1 | Speaker and Listener Skills

Speaker Skills	Listener Skills
1. Asking for reinforcers 2. Asking for "help" 3. Asking for a "break" 4. Answering "no" to "Do you want this?" 5. Answering "yes" to "Do you want this?"	6. Responding to "Wait/No" 7. Responding to transitional cues (going from one activity to another) 8. Following functioning directions (obeying oral or visual instructions) 9. Following a schedule

Assessing Critical Communication Skills

It will be helpful for you to assess each of these critical skills for your child. We suggest that you complete a checklist involving all of these skills no matter what other measures have been done to assess your child's language skills. That is, knowing that your child has a language age-equivalent of a nine-year-old will not necessarily tell you whether he can accomplish each skill independently. At the end of this chapter is a checklist regarding the nine critical skills that you can complete for your child.

For each skill, it will be helpful to think about how your child currently handles a particular situation. For example, when your child sees a toy or something else he wants, what does he do? Is his response appropriate or problematic? If a two-year-old pointed to a book on a shelf that he wanted to look at, that might be considered appropriate for his skill and age level. On the other hand, if he stood and stomped his feet and screamed until someone gave him the book, that would be something you would want to work on.

After you've gone through all nine skills, look at each of the problem areas and rate how difficult each problem is. That is, prioritize the severity of the problems to help determine which ones you'll want to work on first. For example, if your child requests help by handing you items that do not work, but you'd like him to say the word "help," that would not be as important as working on his screaming when he can't get toys that are out of reach.

Critical Communication Skills: Problems and Potential Solutions

When you are analyzing routines and activities that are problematic for your child, as will be discussed in Chapter 7, be sure to consider what role expressive or receptive communication plays in the problem. For children with autism spectrum disorders, lack of appropriate communication skills are often among the biggest impediments to smooth family functioning. When your child is having difficulties with a family activity or routine, ask yourself whether a problem with one or more of these specific communication skills is contributing to the problem.

After you have used the critical communication skills checklist to pinpoint what areas of communication are posing the biggest problem for your child and family, the next step is to figure out what your child can learn to do instead of what he is doing now. The following sections therefore give many examples of potential problems with communication that children with autism have, together with some potential solutions. Once you have identified a skill you would like your child to learn in place of a current problematic communicative behavior, add it to the list of teaching goals you developed while reading Chapter 1. You also will want to review your priorities, in terms of which skills should get the most attention at first. In the next two chapters you will learn strategies to begin teaching these skills to your child.

Requesting Reinforcers

Asking for a desired item is perhaps the most fundamental communication skill. Requesting allows us to get access to items and activities that are essential for day-to-day living or that allow us to enjoy ourselves and our interactions with others. Refer back to Chapter 2 for guidance on choosing and using reinforcers that your child will be motivated to obtain.

> ***Problem:*** *Three-year-old Derek wants to watch his favorite video, but his dad has put it on the top shelf above the television where Derek can't reach it. He tries to climb on top of the television but can't quite make it. He begins whimpering and*

jumping up and down. When Mom comes into the room, not knowing that Dad put the video out of reach, she cannot figure out what he wants.

Potential Solution: Teach Derek to use his PECS system to ask for the video.

Problem: *Eight-year-old Sam wants some juice and the juice carton is empty. He goes to his mother and says, "Sam, say you want some juice."*

Potential Solution: Teach Sam to say, "I want some juice."

Problem: *Twelve-year-old Curt likes Marsha, who is new to the class. He walks over and says, "Hi, can I kiss you?"*

Potential Solution: Teach Curt to say, "Hi, I'm Curt. Can we talk for a minute?"

Problem: *Fourteen-year-old Darlene is about to do some homework. She looks at her sister who is on the computer and says, "Get off now!"*

Potential Solution: Teach Darlene to say to her sister, "I have homework to do. Can I use the computer soon?"

Requesting Assistance

Asking for help is universally important because everyone at some time will be in a situation where the solution to a problem must come from someone else.

Problem: *Joey is playing with his favorite electronic train set. He has learned to set the track up on his own; connect the train engine, cars, and caboose; and put the train on the track and start the train. Today when the train rounds the first corner, it falls off the track. Joey tries several times to restart the train but doesn't notice that the track is not properly connected at the first corner. After several attempts to get the train going, each time ending with a derailed train, Joey screams and throws the train across the room.*

Potential solution: Teach Joey to bring the train to his sister and gesture for help.

Problem: *Amanda is working on her math homework at the kitchen table along with her brother. She carefully adds the numbers for each problem, reciting the problem aloud as she works. ("Seven plus eight equals fifteen.") When her pencil lead breaks, she grabs her brother's pencil.*

Potential solution: Teach Amanda to point to her brother's pencil and say, "Can I use that for now?"

In teaching your child to request help, you will want to identify many activities and times in your child's day when it will be natural for him to ask for help. Table 3-2 lists some common opportunities for teaching children about asking for assistance.

Table 3-2 | "Help" Opportunities

1. Blow bubbles
2. Blow up balloon
3. Put coins in vending machine
4. Cut food
5. Cut paper
6. Insert CD/DVD/ music tape/video
7. Open curtains
8. Open bottle
9. Open doors
10. Open food packets
11. Open milk or juice carton
12. Pour from pitcher/carton
13. Put on shoe/socks
14. Snap clothes/coat
15. Take cap off marker
16. Tie jacket strings/shoelaces
17. Turn on/off lights
18. Turn on/off water
19. Reach towel to dry hands
20. Turn on/off music player/television
21. Unwrap plastic utensils/straw
22. Unzip backpack/coat/pencil pouch
23. Zip backpack/coat/pencil pouch
24. Wind up toy
25. Install batteries

Requesting a Break

We all have been in situations where the demand is too high or fatigue has set in due to the length of the task at hand. In these cases, we ask for a break—some time to recuperate. We periodically need to avoid or escape from certain events and have learned to do so in a number of socially acceptable ways. While parents may be able to "read" when their child needs a break, children also need a calm way to ask for a break on their own. As with learning to ask for help, the key will be for the child to be able to ask for a break before he has a tantrum.

Problem: *Maria's aunt, uncle, and cousins are visiting from out of town. The entire family has congregated in the family room and Maria is sitting in her dad's lap. As all the family members talk at once, trying to catch each other up on their lives, Maria tries to slide out of Dad's lap. When he holds on tight, boosting her back up into his lap, she cries loudly, arches her body backwards, and hits her head into Dad's head.*

Potential solution: Teach Maria to use a break card when she is overwhelmed by a situation. In the future, Maria can hand her father a card that says, "Break" and walk to the break-area.

Problem: *Reggie's parents are having a party and want Reggie to meet their guests. Reggie has learned to greet people by saying, "Hi, nice to meet you." Several guests arrive at once and as Reggie's father and mother introduce him to each guest, he greets them appropriately. As the tenth and eleventh guests arrive, Reggie is reluctant to go to them with his parents, but when his dad firmly guides him, he approaches the new guests and greets them. As the next several guests arrive at the door, Reggie begins to breathe heavily. He greets the first, and then tries to back away. When his dad nudges him forward, Reggie shouts, "Hi, nice to meet you," and pulls away from his father. When Reggie's mother says, "Reggie, say hello to Mr. and Mrs. Wells," Reggie yells, "Hi to meet you!" and runs from the room.*

Potential solution: Teach Reggie to say, "I need to find a quiet place for a moment" when he feels like yelling.

Rejecting

Rejecting offers from other people allows us to participate in interactions with communicative partners who are determining what, specifically, we might want. When we cannot politely or calmly reject something that we don't like, trouble usually ensues.

> **Problem:** *Jacqui, nineteen, is having dinner at her grandparents' house with her parents. She has learned to sit with her family at mealtime, but meals at her house involve Mom or Dad handing her a plate of her favorite foods. Tonight Jacqui's grandmother tries to pass Jacqui the bowl of broccoli. Jacqui won't take it from her and when her grandmother tries to spoon some broccoli onto Jacqui's plate, Jacqui forcefully pushes the bowl away, knocking over her water glass.*
>
> ***Potential solution:*** Teach Jacqui to shake her head "no" when offered foods she does not like.

> ***Problem:*** *Jamie wants to watch a video. Her sister tries to help and puts in the Barney video because it is nearby. Jamie screams "Sesame Street! Sesame Street! Sesame Street!"*
>
> ***Potential solution:*** Jamie learns to say, "No thanks" and give her sister a picture of the video she wants to watch.

Accepting

We all can remember times when we've played "Twenty Questions" with our children in order to figure out what they want. If we are holding out a preferred item and asking, "Do you want this?" most often our children will simply take it. We won't always be able to hold an item ("Do you want to go to the swimming pool?"), so our children need to be able to indicate "yes!"

> ***Problem:*** *Eight-year-old Sierra is in the kitchen with her older brother, Sam. Sam is trying to help his sister get a snack and is pulling one food after another out of the snack cupboard, asking, "Is this what you want?" He thinks it is the blue corn chips she wants, but he hasn't been able to reach them yet. So, without showing them to her he asks, "Do you want the blue*

corn chips?" Sierra doesn't answer. Finally, he reaches them in the back of the cupboard and when he holds them out to Sierra, she takes them from him.

Potential solution: When Sam asks, "Is this what you want?" Sierra nods her head.

Problem: *Fourteen-year-old Alexis is helping her mother make cookies. When it is time to stir the dough, her mother asks, "Do you want the big spoon?" Alexis answers, "Big spoon."*

Potential solution: When asked whether she wants something, Alexis learns to say, "Yes!"

Responding to "Wait" or "No"

What are we trying to communicate to someone when we say, "Wait?" The message is actually complex: "I know what you want and you are going to get it but after some more time." Our children must understand that they are not being denied access to the item—they are eventually going to get it. Because learning to wait is such a crucial skill for everyone, we will provide some more details on the issues that need to be addressed. For a more complete description of effective strategies to promote waiting, please refer to *A Picture's Worth*.

There are three key elements to teaching someone to wait:

First, you must be able to fully control access to whatever it is that person is waiting for. That is, if you can't provide it when you want to, then the lesson will be very difficult to learn. Therefore, start with something you know your child wants but you can give it to him at any time.

Second, you must control how long your child should wait. Start with a time interval that is so short—one or two seconds!—that it virtually guarantees that there will be no failure. Then, begin to gradually increase the time interval. If you add too much time and run into a problem, simply readjust your next interval to something shorter. You may want to highlight that it is time to practice waiting with a visual cue, such as a large, brightly colored card that has 'wait' written on it.

Third, as the wait intervals become one minute or longer, you will want to help your child select something easy to do while waiting. The point is, do not expect someone to simply wait while doing nothing—that remains very hard for all of us! Instead, pick some easy activities such as looking at a picture book or listening to music (as long as he is not waiting to listen to music).

Here are some more common situations that all families face and suggested solutions:

> ***Problem:*** *Mom is on the telephone trying to schedule an appointment. Mark comes up to her and begins tugging on her, trying to get her to move with him. Mom resists and whispers to Mark, "Just a minute. I'm almost done." Mark falls to the floor and begins screaming.*
>
> ***Potential solution:*** Mom teaches Mark to use a Wait card. For example, Mom hands Mark a card that says, "Wait" and Mark calmly stands next to her for one minute. Mom then pays attention to Mark. (Note: Even if Mark can't yet read, he can learn to associate this visually unique card with waiting.)

> ***Problem:*** *Sue's family is planning an outing to a favorite restaurant for dinner. During the early afternoon, Sue begins asking her parents when they're leaving and they answer, "Not for several hours," "Later," or "at 6:00." Sue does not know how to tell time and continues to ask every 15 or 20 minutes, which begins to annoy her parents. By the time the family finally leaves for the restaurant, everyone is frustrated.*
>
> ***Potential solution:*** Her parents place a picture of the restaurant on Sue's picture schedule, which she quietly checks several times during the afternoon.

> ***Problem:*** *Marshall has finished his homework and a bowl of ice cream that he had earned. He asks his dad if he can have another bowl of ice cream. His father says, "No, one is enough." Marshall ignores his dad and heads for the freezer for more ice cream. His father blocks his path and they start to yell and shout at each other.*
>
> ***Potential solution***: Marshall's parents teach him "the no game." They tell Marshall that sometimes they will say "no" to him, but if he responds calmly they will provide other types of rewards—special time with them when he

can pick which game to play. They give Marshall an index card with five open circles and tell him that he will earn a token for each time he calmly responds when they say, "no." When all five circles are filled, he can pick a game to play. At first, Marshall's parents arrange to say "no" at times when it does not seem highly important to Marshall. For instance, he is about to sit on one chair at the dinner table and they say, "No, please sit on that chair." When he follows through, he earns a token. After several weeks of this type of practice, Marshall asks once again for more ice cream. When his father says, "no," he calmly walks out of the kitchen and his father praises him while giving him a token.

Following Directions

Responding to directions is viewed as a critical communication skill because of the potential risks associated with failing to understand a message. For example, when Mom shouts to her son, "Don't walk in front of the swings!" failure to respond could result in injury. As we discussed earlier, we need to first teach our children to respond to directions that will produce meaningful and desired outcomes from our children's points of view.

Problem: *Mom and Dad report that Angela sometimes looks toward them when they call her name. If she's engaged in a favorite activity, however, she doesn't respond when they say, "Come here." She seems to understand directions some of the time but not always. For example, yesterday when Dad told her to put her shoes away, she didn't do so. But this morning as Dad was getting on his coat so they could go to the park, he told her to get her shoes, and she ran right to them.*

Potential solution: Angela's parents can teach her to listen for her name paired with "come here" by rewarding her with favorite items (e.g., toys, snacks, etc.) for coming over.

Following a Schedule

We adults keep track of all the important things we need to do today, this week, or this month by using some type of written calendar system. Children also like to know what is expected of them and when activities will occur. Therefore, we should teach them how to use systems that contain information about their future schedule of activities.

Schedules can come in many shapes and forms. If your child can read, then using words may be helpful, but virtually all children with autism can understand and use pictures or other three-dimensional items to keep track of their schedules. When you use pictures within a schedule, it is a good idea to first teach your child what the pictures mean (i.e., what to do when he sees a picture) and only then teach him how to use the schedule itself. We like to teach one lesson at a time and avoid mixing them together. The pictures you use should refer to important objects, activities, or areas of your home or neighborhood. Your child should be able to respond to the picture without someone telling him what the picture means—otherwise, why use the pictures? For example, when shown a picture of a spoon, your child should know that he should get the spoon and go to the area or start the activity shown without someone saying, "Right! Get the spoon!"

We tend to arrange the pictures in a top-down fashion to show the sequence of events as shown in Figure 1 on the next page, but you can also use notebooks that show a single activity for each page or use some other systematic presentation style. Figure 1 is an example of a vertical schedule that includes different approaches to offering choices to students. Figure 2 is an example of a pocket schedule that a child can take with him into the community or use at home.

For more details on how to teach the use of schedule, you can read either *A Picture's Worth: PECS and Other Visual Communication Strategies in Autism* by Andy Bondy and Lori Frost (Woodbine House, 2002) or *Activity Schedules for Children with Autism* by Lynn E. McClannahan and Patricia Krantz (Woodbine House, 1999). The first book also describes how to introduce important elements such as choice and surprise into these systems.

Problem: *On weekdays, Mom and Dad maintain a very predictable routine in the household. David seems content to follow along with the family activities. On weekends, though, when the schedule is more unpredictable or loosely structured, David has frequent tantrums. On days when any kind of "surprise" occurs (an anticipated trip to the park is cancelled when it storms), David is inconsolable.*

Figure 1: Vertical Schedule with Choices

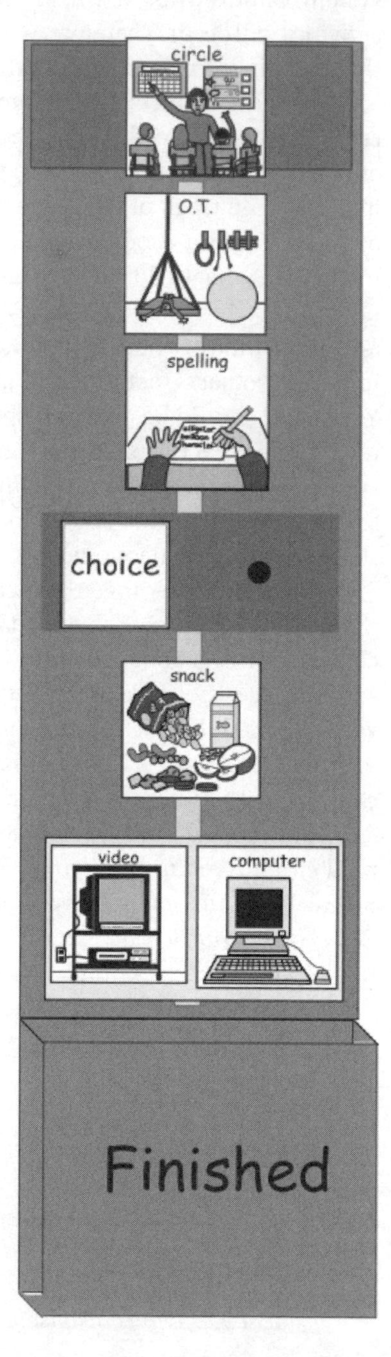

Figure 2: Pocket Schedule

Potential solution: David's parents introduce a "surprise" card on his schedule during weekdays. Initially, they make sure the surprise is something that David enjoys, such as time on the computer. Later, these good surprises are intermixed with surprise activities that David feels neutral about. Finally, his parents intersperse some surprises concerning things that David does not enjoy. Then his parents begin to use a visual schedule for weekends as well.

Dealing with Transitions

Everyone must deal with transitions—between locations, activities, and from person to person. Use of a schedule can help a child understand what is going to happen at different times of the day. However, some children respond to transitions as if their lives were being turned upside down! While you may think that improving information about the upcoming event will reduce the magnitude of the ensuing tantrum, in our experience providing more information (even visually based) is not always sufficient.

Some transitions involve changes from activities that are highly rewarding to those that are less rewarding—and no one looks forward to leaving pleasant activities. Some children become upset even when they are asked to change from a less rewarding activity to one that is more rewarding! We think this may be because the transition involves leaving something behind as well as changing to a new activity. For children with autism spectrum disorders, having information about the next *reward* may be more important than having information about the next *activity*. When the next activity is not inherently rewarding, then adding a separate reinforcer may be necessary.

Problem: *MaryJane has just finished her breakfast and is coloring on a piece of paper in the kitchen. Her mother tells her* *that it is time to play in the family room. MaryJane throws the crayons on the floor, and screams while her mother physically guides her to the family room. Within a few minutes, she is calm once more and contentedly playing with her toys. Then, her mother tells her that it is time to water the plants—something that MaryJane usually enjoys. She screams and throws the toys around while her mother coaxes her to get the watering can. This pattern cycles many times each day.*

Potential solution: MaryJane's mother lets MaryJane know what her reward will be for making a transition before asking her to change activities. For example, while MaryJane is coloring, her mother brings her one of her favorite toys from the family room. She shows the toy to her daughter, who immediately reaches for it. Then she says, "Let's play with the toys in the family room . . . but first we need to put away the crayons." MaryJane puts away the crayons and runs to play with the toy. Later, while MaryJane is still playing with the toy, her mother shows her a picture of the watering can. While she is looking at the picture, her mother says, "Let's go water the plants . . . but first we need to clean up the toys." Throughout the day, MaryJane's mother shows her the next available reward before indicating that she needs to stop what she is currently doing.

Review

This section of the Pyramid Approach has dealt with communication skills. It is extremely important to teach children to use functional communication skills at home and in the community. We've noted several key communication skills and strategies to promote them. When these critical skills are weak or missing, we often see severe behavior problems in their place. Since all families are unique and not all families go into the same community settings, it is crucial that you assess your child's abilities to communicate in the many different settings where your child is expected to participate and then map out a plan to help improve each of the critical skills described in this chapter. Remember that communication is something that you should work on during all activities—we don't suggest having a special time to practice communication. Instead, look for opportunities to work on these skills throughout the day and across all environments. The next chapter will help you learn to build lessons involving functional activities or communication skills into your daily routine.

CRITICAL FUNCTIONAL COMMUNICATION SKILLS CHECKLIST©

Name:		Date:	

Skill	**Example**	**Appropriate?**
1. Request reinforcers		
edibles		
toys		
activities		
2. Request help/assistance		
3. Request break		
4. Reject		
5. Affirm/Accept		
6. Respond to "Wait"		
7. Transition between activities		
8. Respond to directions		
Visual Directions		
Orient to name being signaled		
"Come here"		

"Stop"		
"Sit down"		
"Give it to me"		
"Go get…" (familiar item)		
"Go to…" (familiar location)		
"Put it back/down"		
"Let's go/ Come with me."		
Oral Directions		
Orient to name being shown		
"Come here"		
"Stop"		
"Sit down"		
"Give it to me"		
"Go get…" (familiar item)		
"Go to…" (familiar location)		
"Put it back/down"		
"Let's go/ Come with me."		
9. Follow visual schedule		

4 Creating Natural Opportunities for Learning

Kimberly has been thinking about her son, Daniel, and what she can teach him to help him be more independent in and around the home. She wants him to learn some skills that are relatively simple, such as using the buttons to turn on his TV or computer, pointing to a drink in the refrigerator and saying, "Apple juice," putting his dirty cup in the sink, etc. She also would like him to learn more complex skills—putting toothpaste on his toothbrush and brushing all his teeth reasonably well; setting the table for the entire family at dinner time; looking at a picture-array of items to buy in the supermarket and putting them all in the cart. Kimberly expects Daniel to respond to her requests to start certain activities but she also wants him to initiate some of these activities so that she doesn't feel as if she is running his life. How can she begin to plan to use everyday activities to create learning opportunities for Daniel?

We advocate using many common activities around the home and neighborhood to create natural opportunities for learning. While children learn many important skills at school, there are some skills that are unique to the home and neighborhood that are virtually impossible to replicate at school. And, many of the skills learned at school need to be used at home. Schools are a time-limited resource, while children will live in a home-like setting for the rest of their lives. Parents can be excellent teachers without making their homes into a school. In this chapter, we will look at how to find many opportunities to teach your child within your home and your particular community. Your child will need to learn different types of activities and skills and thus you will need to design different types of lessons. We will describe some of the most common issues related to designing effective lessons and provide examples of how they can be incorporated into everyday routines.

Discrete Lessons

Some activities are relatively short and sweet. That is, they begin with a simple instruction or request, and are followed by reasonably straightforward tasks. For example, you could ask your daughter to come to you, bring you a fork, wipe her nose with a tissue, or tell you the name of a toy that you're holding. Each time your child succeeds, she receives praise and possibly some other simple reward. Notice that the form or type of response is not at issue—the correct response can involve doing something or communicating about something. We call these direct, straightforward types of lesson *discrete trials*. In this case, *discrete* means distinct, separate, or isolated, while *trial* is synonymous with opportunity.

You will recognize that schools are filled with discrete trial types of lessons—rote learning about math facts, names of country or state capitals, and names of objects or their attributes are all examples of this type of lesson. The age of the student does not determine whether or not a lesson involves a discrete trial; high schools students and preschoolers alike learn many discrete trial lessons. In fact, higher levels of education often involve greater amounts of rote learning—for instance, all the elements on the periodic table, all the states and their capitals, all the presidents, etc. So, when you read our discussion of discrete trials, please do not think that this involves a special kind of lesson for children with autism or other learning difficulties. Everyone needs to learn many different discrete trial lessons at school, home, and in the community.

Consider some of the most common discrete trial types of lessons for children to learn at home, as listed in Table 4-1 on the next page. Also consider examples of discrete lessons our children need to learn in the community, as listed in Table 4-2.

The Role of Repetition in Teaching Discrete Skills

When you have identified discrete skills for your child to learn at home, you also need to identify many opportunities for your child to

Table 4-1 | Discrete Activities at Home

Area	Discrete Trial Activity
Kitchen	Respond to "Give me the spoon"
Bedroom	Kiss Dad goodnight
Living Room	Point to picture in book Mom is reading
Dining Room	Ask for drink
Bathroom	Choose toothbrush
Backyard	Kick a ball

Table 4-2 | Discrete Activities in the Community

Area	Discrete Trial Activity
Mall	Throw a coin in fountain
Grocery Store	Point to desired cereal
Playground	Ask for swing
Neighbor's house	Greet adults and children
Library	Choose from three books offered by Mom
Haircut	Take lollipop from bowl
Dentist's office	Respond to "Open up!"

practice those skills. But you have to make sure that in repeating a skill you are not actually reducing the likelihood that your child will learn it. This may happen if you remove your child's motivation to perform the skill or ask her to over-practice it. You also want to arrange for the skill to be repeated in a natural way that makes sense to your child.

Does Repetition Fit the Situation?

In general, we all know that repetition is often beneficial to learning. If I want to learn to be good at shooting foul-shots in basketball, shooting the ball one time per week will not lead to much improvement. But, while we know that practice may help, it is not always easy to know how much repetition we should plan for at any one time.

In fact, sometimes repetition may be counterproductive to the goal of enhancing the likelihood of learning. Imagine an interaction with your daughter, who, for the first time in her life, says, "Slide" while standing by the backdoor and pointing to the slide that she obviously wants to play on. Would you say, "Great! Go outside," but when she took one step out the door, pull her back inside and immediately say, "Now say it again!" We think everyone will recognize that such a tactic would be effective if we want the child to have a tantrum but this type of repetition will not help her learn to ask to go outside. Instead, she should immediately go to play on the slide as a powerful reward for using functional communication indicating what she wants. Although we will want to plan for other similar occasions to encourage and support her efforts to speak, asking her to immediately repeat her request will not be beneficial.

How Many Repetitions Should You Do?

In situations where repetition would be helpful, how many opportunities should we create right now? As we noted earlier, you may have observed teachers at school taking data on each trial and arranging for a block of 10 trials. Why 10? It would be nice if research supported that this number is the best number of repetitions to promote learning, but unfortunately, there is no such data. In fact, people tend to use 10 trials so that they can quickly determine the percent correct per block of trials—after all, it's easy to see that 7 out of 10 is 70 percent. However, most of us are not equally adept at immediately seeing that 8 out of 11 trials is about 73 percent. To avoid the more difficult math issue, many people arrange for a block of 10 trials. While this may make some aspects of a teacher's life easier, it is not being done to make the lesson more effective. The prime difficulty for teachers and parents alike is that there is no magic number of repetitions to be used for all lessons involving discrete trials.

Furthermore, at some point in a lesson, continued repetitions may lead to students changing their correct answers. Why would someone stop giving the correct answer? It may have to do with the child's perspective, which may be different than our own. Let me share an observation that we made in a classroom for children with autism. It was 10 o'clock in the morning. On the teacher's list of one-step directions (a type of discrete trial lesson) was the instruction, "Go get your lunchbox." So, the teacher said this to George, who immediately ran across the room, put his hand on his lunchbox, and turned to smile at the teacher. She smiled back and said, "Good! Come sit down." It is very likely that the teacher thought that her praise was a good reward for George (and in many other situations, it was). When he sat down, the teacher said, "Go get your lunchbox." Again, George zoomed across the room, and smiled while placing his hand on his lunchbox. The teacher smiled and said, "Good. Come here and sit down!" Faithfully, George did as he was told. Once seated, the teacher said, "Go get your lunchbox." This time, George sauntered across the room, put his hand on his lunchbox, and looked at the teacher without smiling. She did smile and said, "Good! Sit over here!" He sat down. You guessed it—she said, "Go get your lunchbox." And George once again slowly walked to his lunchbox.

Although you do not know this teacher, I'm sure you have a good idea of how many times she intended to ask George to get his lunchbox. Right! Her data form had ten boxes and she was planning to run that number of trials. Around trial number seven, when she issued her instruction, George walked across the room and put his hand on a flowerpot sitting on the window sill and looked back at the teacher with a rather inquisitive look. Although we don't profess to be able to read minds, we're sure he was thinking something along the lines of, "Maybe today, *this* is the lunchbox because *that* can't be the lunchbox or she wouldn't keep asking me to get it!"

In other words, George may have focused on getting to eat lunch as the natural reward for getting his lunchbox. Since that did not happen, even though the teacher smiled and praised him, he most likely thought he was not being successful. One strategy that many of us use when learning new skills is called "lose-shift"—if something isn't working, try something else! In this situation, the teacher's repetition was convincing George that something was wrong; his answers were not leading to getting to eat lunch. Therefore, when we want to use repetition to help build up "learning muscles," we want to make sure that the number of repetitions fits the situation.

For example, you may want your daughter to put a napkin next to each plate at dinnertime. Clearly, putting 10 napkins by each plate won't help, nor would setting the table for 10 (unless that's your family size!). On the other hand, you may want your 5-year-old child to sort her socks from those of her 6-foot 5-inch dad's socks. In this case, the number of socks to sort will be related to how many socks you've washed—maybe Dad has 6 pairs and your child has 7 pairs. (When you start this lesson, you may want to be sure there are only a few socks and only add more as your child becomes more acquainted with the task.)

In short, you need to decide before you start a lesson whether repetition will fit into the situation, and if so, how many meaningful opportunities you want to provide during each occasion. You may need to make adjustments over time—your child may really enjoy the task and you then may want to extend how long it takes to complete the job. On the other hand, your child may not enjoy the task or may become readily bored. If providing additional motivation to complete the task does not seem to be very effective, then you may want to reduce the number of repetitions you are requiring for that job.

How do we ensure enough repetitions for activities that don't naturally seem "repeatable?" For George in the example above, the teacher could use naturally occurring opportunities for repetition by spreading the "Get your lunchbox" direction across the day. The first opportunity occurs just before lunch. The next opportunity could be just after lunch when George needs to retrieve his lunchbox before leaving the cafeteria. Finally, at the end of the day, George's teacher might give the direction once more while George is gathering his belongings to take home. At home, you can create multiple "natural" opportunities for putting napkins on the table by having your son or daughter put out one or two napkins for breakfast, afternoon snack, and dinner.

Sequential Lessons

While there are virtually innumerable discrete trial opportunities, not all lessons in life involve simple, brief actions. Some of what we must learn involves actions that require many steps to be performed in a particular order. For example, you may think of "getting dressed" as a single action, but in fact, getting dressed involves many steps where the order of the steps is important. Not only do children need different actions to put on their socks versus shoes, but they also need to learn to put on their socks before they put on their shoes. We will describe lessons that require many ordered steps as *sequential* to remind ourselves that we are dealing with a sequence of actions to be learned.

There are many sequential lessons in and around the home, and many more to learn in the neighborhood. We also should point out that sequential tasks may change over time—that is, as a child gets older and acquires more skills, we often make adjustments to what we expect a child (or adult) to do. So, grocery shopping for a 5-year-old will often involve fewer skills than what we would expect of a 15-year-old.

Let's review some common sequential lessons around the home as noted in Table 4-3. You also should consider addressing some of the sequential lessons noted in Table 4-4 that occur in common community locales.

Table 4-3 | Sequential Lessons at Home

Area	Sequential Lesson Activity
Kitchen	Sort silverware while unloading dishwasher
Bedroom	Get dressed
Living Room	Choose, load, and play a video
Dining Room	Set the table
Bathroom	Wash hands
Backyard	Plant seeds

Table 4-4 | Sequential Lessons in the Community

Area	Sequential Lesson Activity
Mall	Order a meal
Grocery Store	Empty shopping cart onto checkout belt
Playground	Build in the sandbox
Neighbor's house	Make a snack
Library	Check out a book
Haircut	Sing the "Haircut" song
Dentist's office	Brush teeth

How Do Communication Goals Relate to the Type of Lesson?

As with any skill, communication goals can either be discrete or sequential. For expressive communication skills (whether involving speech, sign, PECS, or other modalities), examples of discrete lessons would include answering simple questions, such as, "What's your dog's name?"; "What do you want for dinner?"; or "Who is playing in the den?" For receptive communication skills (whether responding to spoken or visually based instructions), examples of discrete lessons would include appropriately responding to "Bring me the hammer," "You can turn on the TV now," and "Give this to your dad."

Examples of sequential lessons involving expressive communication would include responding to "Tell me how to set the table" or "Tell me about your class schedule." Furthermore, getting children to respond in sentences as opposed to single words (via speech, pictures, signs, or otherwise) also involves using chains of responses and are thus sequential lessons. Examples of sequential lessons involving receptive skills include, "Bring me two spoons, and put two plates on the table." "Hang up your coat and then you can go watch TV."

In the next chapter, we will discuss how and when to use prompts when teaching a lesson. All of these considerations apply to communications lessons, just as they do with any other type of lesson. It may be difficult to think about avoiding verbal prompts during communications lessons, especially subtle ones (such as, "Use a whole sentence...") because they do not involve much effort on our part, but they still need to be removed to prevent prompt-dependency from creeping into the situation. (See Chapter 5.)

Designing a Task Analysis

A sequential lesson involves teaching many steps in a set order. Therefore, it is important to note the specific steps and the order in which you expect them to occur. Formally, we would call this a *task analysis* (TA), but it is exactly the same process as writing down the recipe for something we plan to make for dinner. Although I don't always follow a recipe for everything I cook, if I want to make cheesecake exactly the way my mother used to make it, then I should follow a specific and detailed recipe. When we want someone to learn to perform a complex, sequential task independently, then we will need to be consistent with the steps and their order.

How can parents design a good task analysis (TA)? When you realize that the skill you want to teach involves a sequence of steps, then you will need to plan out each of those steps. As we've noted before, there are no perfect lessons, so there are no perfect task analyses. There are many effective ways to make a bed (despite what your mother told you!), or to get dressed, or even to open a hard-boiled egg (read *Gulliver's Travels* for more on that!). We suggest you use the following guidelines when you want to design your own TA:

1. Form a little group within your family and talk about how you each perform whatever task you are aiming to teach. Most likely, you will find some variations on how to do any task. Try and come to a reasonable compromise on how best for your child to perform the task. You can think of this as a type of armchair exercise because most of this step will be done by just talking about the activity.
2. Watch how someone performs the task and see how well it matches your written description. Rewrite as necessary to best describe what you see rather than what someone tells you he or she is doing. It may be helpful to watch more than one person perform the task.
3. Talk to your school team (or other families) and see if anyone has written a version of a TA for this activity. You do not have to accept what someone else wrote without considering modifications to fit your child and situation.
4. Consider how your child's skills and age may affect your expectations. For example, you would expect more from a teenager cleaning her room than you would a 4-year-old, so the TAs would be different for each child. If your child can read instructions, then a TA may involve steps that would not be the same as for a child who cannot read.
5. Test out your TA! First, test it on someone other than your child—a friend, perhaps, or a sibling. See if they can read your TA and follow it in the manner you expect.
6. Then try it with your child. That is, watch carefully as you use the TA to teach your child and be prepared to

make modifications. Your child can teach you a lot about how she learns best, so take advantage of her advice!

The steps in your TA are put together much like a chain—each step is like a loop linked to the step before and the step after. In the next chapter we will describe how to use prompts to best teach sequential lessons, and even consider which end of the chain you will want to start teaching.

Now let's consider some common sequential lessons at home and in the neighborhood. At home, the task analysis for washing hands might look like this:

1. Turn on water
2. Adjust temperature
3. Wet hands
4. Dispense soap onto hands
5. Rub hands
6. Rinse hands
7. Turn water off
8. Dry hands

In the community, the task analysis for checking a book out from the library could look like this:

1. Choose book
2. Walk to checkout counter
3. Wait in line
4. Put book on counter
5. Give librarian library card
6. Take book back from librarian
7. Leave checkout line

Before you set out to teach your child the steps you have identified in a task analysis, you will need to decide which step to teach first. This is covered in the next chapter, on Teaching Strategies.

Who Goes First?

When our children are young, we are accustomed to asking—or simply telling—them what to do. We are the ones in charge and set up situations such as when to set the table, when the TV can be on, when it's time to take a bath, and so on. We often ask many questions, such as "What do you want to drink?"; "Which video do you want to watch?"; "Did you have fun at school today?" or even, "Look at me (so I can wash your dirty face!)." As parents, we are used to taking the lead for our children. But as they get older and more competent, we like to see our children become increasingly independent. When our daughter is 3, we'll happily make her favorite cheese sandwich, but when she's 15, we expect her to be able to make her own sandwich (even if we still have to clean up after her!). Furthermore, even when children are quite young, there are times we would like to see them be spontaneous rather than having to play "20 Questions" to find out what they want.

In other words, we need to strike a balance between teaching our children to follow our directions some of the time and yet be independent at other times. In the next chapter we will describe how we might go about teaching these different styles but for now we want to focus on finding situations in which the different styles are easily identified. When choosing between teaching a lesson that will result in a child being responsive as opposed to spontaneous, it will not matter whether the lesson involves discrete or sequential activities. It also will not matter whether the lesson will involve communication as opposed to physical routines. Each of these can be either responsive or self-initiated.

For example, we could teach a child to set the table (a sequential task) only when we say, "Go set the table." On the other hand, we could aim for the child to learn to set the table at 6:00 P.M., independent of what we've said. Likewise, we could teach a child to turn the TV on (a discrete action) only when we say, "It's time for television" or we could teach her how to turn the TV on whenever she wants to watch a show or video.

When teaching social or communication skills, we need to make similar choices. We can teach a child to say, "Hello" only when we say hello first, or we can teach the child to initiate the social greeting when entering a room. Our point is that you must decide before you start the lesson what you want the child to do:

1. respond to something you've said or done, or
2. initiate the act following something going on inside of her (e.g., she's hungry) or something around her (e.g., she sees a friend she wants to play with).

It would be nice for us as teachers and parents to be able to teach children to respond to us now and to become more spontaneous on their own later on. Unfortunately, this rarely happens—children with autism tend to become more independent and spontaneous only when we teach (and thus support) them for doing so. Therefore, when you are initially planning a lesson, it is wise to think ahead about not only how you will teach your child to do the skill on your instruction, but also how you will later get her to do it more independently. Many of these issues relate to how to use and phase out prompts, which is discussed in the next chapter.

Building and Taking Advantage of Routines

If you want to learn to teach your child needed skills during the course of everyday life, you will naturally need to learn how to embed teaching in your daily routines. If you need to do a routine anyway, and if one of the steps of the routine involves your child, then whenever you do the routine you will automatically be teaching your child. We can teach any kind of skill in the course of performing a routine, but we will illustrate how to do this with communication skills because all children with autism have needs in this area.

Parents typically understand the advantages of helping their children expand their communication repertoires—both in terms of the total number of words in their vocabulary and in the complexity of their sentence constructions. Parents often observe teachers and speech-language pathologists teaching lessons at school where they try to increase a student's vocabulary by introducing novel items either directly or via pictures. During some of these lessons, a teacher may show the student many common objects, including items that are familiar to the child as well as a few new items around which the lesson is built. For example, we could place a fork, knife, and a spoon before the student and ask her to name each one. Then we could show her a can opener and teach her the name of that item. In this way, the new item is embedded within a relatively easy task. Hopefully, when the child next sees a can opener at home, she will be able to recall the name learned at school. Sometimes, this lesson is arranged using pictures or photographs of both the familiar as well as the novel items.

Keeping with our theme that parents can arrange for successful lessons at home without changing their home into a classroom, let us consider some strategies that we can use at home to help children increase their vocabularies. Our key suggestion involves designing activities and routines to help the child understand the functional value of increasing her vocabulary.

Let's consider this goal with the can opener. Although it is possible to teach a child the name of something and then later learn the use of that object, it is often more effective to first teach the functional use of the item before designing a communication lesson associated with that item. So, at home, we would first create an activity during which a can opener will be helpful. Let's assume that your daughter likes soup and that there are some canned soups that she enjoys. Rather than simply preparing the soup for her—that is, serving hot soup in a bowl—we will first teach her the routine associated with opening the can before preparing the soup. Even children who are too young to manipulate the can opener themselves can learn this routine.

To design an effective routine, we first need to think about the steps that make up the routine. Look at the list below for an example of a task analysis for preparing canned hot soup:

1. Get a bowl
2. Get a spoon
3. Get the can of soup
4. Get the can opener
5. Open the can of soup with the can opener
6. Pour the soup into the bowl
7. Place the lid into the empty can and throw in garbage
8. Put bowl in microwave
9. Turn on microwave for 1 minute
10. Take out bowl and put on table
11. Eat soup with spoon
12. When finished with soup, put bowl and spoon in sink

We hope you can see that this is only *one* way to prepare canned soup! For our example, it is important to note where the can opener will be used—in step 5. When we first begin this lesson, we should not expect the child to actively participate in any single part of the routine. That is, we expect to guide the child throughout the routine. For this kind of activity, which involves many physical actions, we suggest using direct physical assistance. We will eventually have to remove our guidance (see the discussion about getting rid of teaching prompts in Chapter 5). Therefore, we do not want to use many different types of prompts at this point. So, once we announce the general activity ("OK, let's make soup!") in some manner, we would help the child get each of the items we need for the routine. When we have all the items, then we would guide the child to pick up the can opener and place it on the soup can.

Again, whether our aim is to teach the child to independently open the can will be a function of the child's age and skill level. However, our immediate goal is to teach the child to pick up the can opener to begin Step 5. Over several opportunities to make soup, we try to gradually remove our help until the child is automatically picking up the can opener when it is time to use it. Of course, we hope that you will remember to heap great praise upon your child when you see her acquiring that skill! After a few successful opportunities with this step in place, we are ready to create our communication lesson.

During the next soup-making opportunity, you put the can opener somewhere that your child cannot reach it by herself. Essentially, you place yourself between the child and the completion of the next step. That intervention creates the need for your child to communicate with you in order to complete the routine that she has previously learned. If you tried this arrangement on the very first day of this lesson, she would have no reason to ask for the can opener since she has no idea why she should want it. And, it is not enough to just teach the name of something—we must create the need for communication.

One way to help identify functional vocabulary is to fill out a form like the one shown in Table 4-5.

Note from the table above that you can teach a variety of vocabulary words by varying which item is missing when your child wants to make soup. On some days the can opener is missing and on some days the bowl is missing. In order to balance your child's opportunities for being independent at making soup with her opportunities to learn to communicate while making soup, remember that on some days, no items should be missing.

Review

This chapter introduced the Pyramid Approach to designing effective lessons in various environments. Not all lessons are alike. Some

Table 4-5 | Vocabulary within Routines Form

Routine: Making canned soup

Steps	Vocabulary for Requesting
1. Get a bowl	1. bowl
2. Get a spoon	2. spoon
3. Get the can of soup	3. soup
4. Get the can opener	4. can opener
5. Open the can of soup with the can opener	
6. Pour the soup into the bowl	
7. Place the lid into the empty can and throw can in garbage	7. garbage can
8. Put bowl in microwave	
9. Turn on microwave for 1 minute	9. help
10. Take out bowl and put on table	
11. Eat soup with spoon	
12. When finished, put bowl and spoon in sink	

Reinforcement for completing routine: Getting to eat soup!

are relatively simple and require a single action—these lessons can be described as discrete. Other lessons involve many steps in a particular order—these are sequential lessons. For lessons involving many steps, it will be helpful to write out the task analysis you think will be effective for your child. For either type of lesson, you must consider how to incorporate repetition to promote success but not undermine the power of naturally occurring rewards. Furthermore, you must also consider whether you want the lesson to begin with your action or be initiated by your child. Each decision you make regarding the type of lesson you want your child to learn will affect how you will go about teaching that lesson—the topic of our next chapter.

5 Teaching Strategies for the Home and Community

Lisa and Charles are watching their son Albert as he struggles to put together his train set. They have set a goal of teaching him to do this independently so that he can play while they attend to chores around the house. They know that they need to teach a sequential lesson, since there are several steps involved in connecting the trains. They're not sure, however, how best to help him. Should they point to where the trains connect or just tell him what to do? Is there a way to teach him without having to physically guide him through the right actions? Should they show him a completed set or have him watch them while they put it together? Lisa and Charles wonder whether helping Albert this time will mean that he will come to rely upon them in the future rather than figuring it out for himself. How should they reduce how much help they are giving him? They also aren't sure how to reward him—they know Albert likes to play with the trains, but should they praise him as well? Will that distract him?

Lisa and Charles are struggling with issues that face everyone trying to teach a new skill, whether at home or at school. In addition, they have heard that it is important for children with autism to experience few, if any errors, when learning. Is there a way to teach that will minimize errors and yet not result in the child becoming dependent upon his parents' help? Like most people, they have heard about trial-and-error learning but wonder whether this would be a good strategy for their son—wouldn't this lead to many errors? (In fact, one prominent behavior analyst, Dr. Beth Sulzer-Azaroff, reminds us to practice "*trial and success*" rather than trial-and-error. Careful attention to how we design lessons will result in few errors and effective learning.)

Like Lisa and Charles, you may think that teaching children with autism is hard, or may not know where to begin. The whole idea of keeping your child from making any errors also may seem very intimidating. We believe, however, that parents and other family members are very capable of teaching their children new skills at home and in the community. This chapter will tell you how to begin.

What Is Teaching All About?

Before we focus on what teaching is all about, let's review what it means *to learn*. If you've taught a successful lesson to your child, then your child can do something when the lesson is completed that he or she could not independently accomplish earlier. That is, as teachers, we only know if our children have learned a lesson if we see them doing something different after the lesson than they could do before—they then can "show us what they know."

When we start a lesson, the child cannot perform the lesson goal. In the example above, Albert cannot put his trains together. Let's consider how Albert's parents can teach him to put his trains together. What will Lisa need to do on the first day that she attempts to teach him this skill? If she simply watches him, he will stand there and not accomplish the task. Lisa will have to help her son put the trains together on this day, although her goal is to teach him to play independently, even if she is not in the room. Therefore, one way to think about this (and most) lessons is that the teacher (Lisa) must help the child (Albert) at the start of the lesson but then must stop helping while the child continues to perform the target skill. When the child is independent, he will be responding to *natural cues* in the surroundings—such as the train itself, the tracks for the trains, etc.

Prompts

How can Lisa help Albert on the first day? We immediately recognize that there are many potential ways of helping. Each strategy of help is called a *prompt*. A prompt is simply something that a teacher uses within a lesson to help the child perform the target skill. For example:

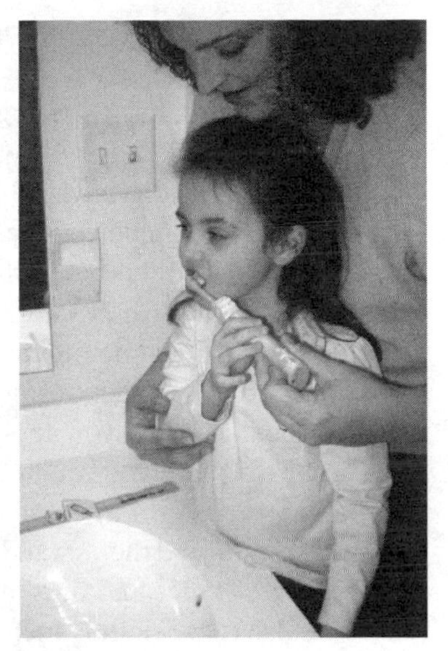

- Lisa could tell her son to pick up the train. That would be a type of ***vocal*** or ***verbal prompt.*** Lisa knows, however, that Albert has a very limited receptive vocabulary, so she isn't sure that he will understand what she is saying. Her words would probably not be an effective prompt because it would not be helpful to Albert.
- Lisa could try to point to the train—thus, trying a type of ***gestural prompt.*** In this case, Lisa knows that Albert rarely looks at what she is pointing to and thus does not choose to try this strategy.
- Lisa could show Albert what to do—thus, trying to ***model*** certain actions that he can then imitate. But Lisa knows that Albert's schoolteachers are still trying to teach him to imitate so she doubts her modeling will be effective right now.
- Lisa could hold up a picture of the train—thus, trying a type of ***visual prompt.*** Here, too, Lisa realizes that her son does not yet seem to always associate pictures that are shown to him with objects around him.
- Finally, Lisa realizes that she can physically guide Albert's hands to put the train together—thus, trying a type of ***physical prompt.*** She knows that this will be effective because her son has accepted her assistance when she has physically helped him with other simple tasks.

Eliminating Prompts

Once Lisa has selected the prompt she will use—in this case, physical assistance—she now needs a strategy to get rid of the prompt.

That is, she must plan to reduce how much physical help she provides so that over time Albert will not need any physical or other prompts to complete putting his trains together.

There are many effective ways to get rid of a prompt. First, Lisa could reduce how much physical help she provides over successive opportunities. For example, for each new car that Albert is trying to add to the train, she could provide slightly less assistance. We would call this "*fading*" a physical prompt, or using *graduated guidance*. There are several ways that prompts can be faded. For physical prompts, such as guiding a child's hand movements, you can gradually decrease how much physical pressure you apply over successive opportunities. You also can alter where you touch the child—you can start with hand-over-hand and then gradually adjust your point of contact to the child's hand, wrist, arm, and then shoulder. The key is to continue to gradually reduce the assistance and thus move the child toward independence.

Lisa also could slightly increase the amount of time she waits between handing Albert a train car and providing physical assistance. We call this strategy "*delayed prompting*." This strategy is often a good choice when you are sure that your prompt will work because on every opportunity, the child succeeds—either on his own or with the prompt.

There are many strategies to eliminate and reduce prompts—far too many for us to review them all here. Each is designed to help a child learn to respond to natural cues rather than teacher prompts. For more information about these strategies we encourage you to read *The Pyramid Approach to Education* (Bondy and Sulzer-Azaroff, 2002—especially Chapter 9).

Are Some Prompts Better Than Others?

By definition, a prompt is something you do or modify within a lesson that successfully helps your child perform the particular skill you are focusing on. Some people prefer using vocal prompts; they like to talk to the child almost continuously. Other people prefer using picture and other visual prompts; they put pictures and signs on everything, everywhere in the home. It is not possible to determine which prompt is "better" than another prompt. If it works, great!

A bigger challenge than finding a prompt that works is selecting a strategy that will remove the prompt. I may find using verbal prompts so easy to use that I forget to plan to remove them. Or, I may put so many pictures around the house that I forget that they won't be in other homes or locations. If I use a series of pictures to prompt a child to get dressed when I am first teaching him that skill, it is my responsibility to recognize that these pictures will later need to be faded. I need to remember that it is possible for my child to learn to get dressed without the pictures (or some other prompt) and I need to plan a strategy to reach that independent goal.

What Do We Do If a Prompt Is Not Effective?

Once you have decided what type of lesson you want to teach—discrete vs. sequential, for example—you then select the type of prompt to use: vocal, physical, gestural, etc. Then you choose a strategy to eliminate the prompt. It is important to remember that not all plans will work and that no one can guarantee that the selected strategy will be effective. At best, we are making educated guesses! Prompts are things we introduce into a lesson that help the child perform the task. If the strategy is not helpful, then it is not really a prompt.

If you point to a picture to help your child pick it up but he does not pick up the picture, then what you did was not really a prompt. In this case, you would need to find another way to help your child—something that will act as a prompt. Likewise, it is possible that when you try to use physical guidance to help your child, he resists and pulls his arm away. In this case, your physical guidance was not a prompt. Perhaps shining a light on the object will draw your child's attention to the object, leading him to pick it up. In this case, the light is a prompt. Essentially, you will not know whether something is a prompt until you try it out and see if it helps your child. So, be willing to be flexible and try out different types of prompts for different lessons.

Should We Combine Prompts?

While Lisa is choosing which prompt to use with her son, she wonders whether it would be better to use several prompts at the same time. That is, should she show him what to do (perhaps using photographs) while she simultaneously tells him what to do as she guides him in what to do? After all, it seems logical that the more help she provides, the more likely Albert is to complete the task. However, she realizes that the goal of her lesson is to eliminate all prompts so that

Albert can play with his trains independently. She knows that if she uses three or four prompts at the same time, she will then need to plan to get rid of all of these prompts. It will be hard enough to eliminate one prompt! More is not always better. So, she wisely plans to use the physical prompts that she knows will be effective and designs a plan to eliminate that single type of prompt.

Charles understands the need to get rid of helpful prompts, but he is concerned that if they do not talk to Albert while he is learning to put his train together, he will not learn any language associated with the task. He wonders if they will need to remain totally silent throughout the lesson. Lisa points out that prompts are actions teachers use before the child tries an action, and while she does not want to combine prompts, she too wants Albert to hear their words in hopes that he will learn to associate them with the activity. So, she rightly advises that they can talk to Albert while he is doing a prompted step (or just after) rather than talk during the prompt itself. Lisa will guide Albert to connect two trains and then immediately say something along the lines of, "Yes! You put the trains together!" or "Wow! Look at the trains! They are together now!" Charles now understands that it is not about *whether* to speak or not; it is more about the timing of what he will say while teaching his son.

Can We Use Prompts When Addressing Challenging Behavior?

In Chapter 8, we discuss the importance of teaching alternative behaviors to replace challenging behaviors you are targeting in your teaching efforts. Part of that overall strategy may involve prompting your child to engage in the alternative behavior, and we will now discuss some issues related to this use of prompts.

One important issue concerns when to prompt your child to do the alternative behavior. We do not think it is a good idea to try to teach any skill when a child is in the midst of a tantrum. During a tantrum, the goal is to calm things down and avoid injuries or serious property damage. However, you should be attentive to what may have triggered the reaction.

Ideally, you would read your child's cues and prompt him *before* he has a tantrum. For example, let's say your child is still in the process of learning to give you items that are not working correctly rather than getting down on the floor and screaming until you help him. To help your son learn the new skill, you need to create situations that lead to him needing help—for example, you can give him a bottle that is closed too tightly for him to open. After you've handed him the bottle but before he screams (possibly within a second or two of struggling with the bottle top), you would arrange for his sister to prompt him (with physical guidance) to hand the bottle to you. You would then say, "Oh, you need help!" and immediately open the bottle. Notice that the prompt from his sister came before any meltdown and not in the middle of screaming. Over opportunities, you would get his sister to gradually reduce the amount of physical assistance she provides.

If you prompt your child once he starts screaming, that is likely to reward him for both screaming and handing you the bottle. Thus, he's likely to repeat the scream the next time a similar situation arises.

Where Should We Start Sequential Lessons?

Whether we are teaching a discrete type of lesson or one that involves many steps, our overall strategy typically involves finding an effective prompt and then eliminating it. In Chapter 4 we discussed the importance of writing down a task analysis for sequential lessons. Once this is completed you still need to decide which end of the sequence you want to teach first. When we start by trying to teach the first step, we describe this as *forward chaining.* For example, you put a puzzle form before your child and you then teach him to put in the first piece, and then another, and another . . . until all the pieces are correctly placed. Another way to teach a sequence is to first teach the last steps—a process described as *backward chaining.*

At first, backward chaining may sound counterintuitive, but there are many examples in our lives when we naturally use this strategy. Think about teaching your daughter to ride a bicycle. Most likely, you helped her get on the bike, supported her while she put her feet on the pedals, helped her start to move the bike, and finally—when she seemed to have balance and a steady speed—you let go! In this case, the first thing she learned was the very last step—keeping the bike moving ahead. The last thing she learned was how to get on the bicycle without help and start to pedal.

Backward chaining is a strategy that we often suggest when teaching the steps of a task analysis. In our puzzle example, if we were using backward chaining, we would put in all of the pieces except the last one and then help the child put that piece in. Once he has learned to put in that piece, then we put in all the pieces except the last two. Once he's put in the second to the last piece, he can complete the puzzle since he's already learned about the last piece. In general, it is the last piece that is nearest in time to completion of the puzzle and thus may be the most rewarding piece of all.

We can use backward chaining in many routines around the house, such as the one in Table 5-1.

Table 5-1 | The Last Step of Sequential Activities

Area	Activity	Last step
Bedroom	Folding clothes	Top half of T-shirt over bottom half
Bedroom	Tying sneaker laces	Pull both loops tight
Kitchen	Making PB&J sandwich	Put bread slices together
Laundry room	Putting wet clothes in dyer	Taking last item in washer and placing in dyer
Family room	Operating (and loading) a DVD player	Pushing the "Play" button
Garden	Fill and use watering can	Pour water on plants

Can We Teach without Prompting?

A major concern about using prompts to help children learn skills is that they will learn to rely upon the prompt, or become *prompt dependent*. Some people assume that prompt dependency is a common feature of children with autism. However, we think that since it is the teacher who selects and uses the prompt, then it is the teacher's responsibility to remove that prompt. In part, that is why we suggest using only one prompt at a time—if you pile them up, then you will have a great deal of work to do to eliminate them all! Whenever we teach using prompts, then we will have to eliminate those prompts.

Fortunately, there are several effective teaching strategies that do not involve prompts and we will discuss these in the next section.

Shaping

The best-known teaching strategy that does not involve using prompts focuses instead on the power of rewards to teach new skills. One of the founders of behavior analysis, B. F. Skinner, described this strategy as *shaping*. In this strategy, the teacher gradually changes the standards for reward, thus encouraging very small adjustments in performance—which, over time, can result in a large behavioral change. For example, Rayna wants to teach her daughter, Doris, to go from dot to dot on a piece of paper using a pencil. She could use physical prompts to guide Doris's actions. Instead, she puts two dots very close together—so close that almost any drawing motion will connect the two.

As soon as Doris draws from one dot to the other, Rayna claps her hands and praises her daughter. Now, Rayna starts gradually to increase the distance between the dots, in increments that are so slight that Doris does not notice the change from opportunity to opportunity. Fairly soon, the dots are inches apart and Doris thinks it's a great game to see where her mother will place the next dot. Notice that Rayna did not use any type of prompt and therefore she did not have to remove any prompts. She did have to very carefully watch her daughter so that she could reward her correct efforts immediately. On any occasion when Doris did not connect the dots, Rayna simply provided another opportunity— sometimes reducing the distance between the dots to improve the likelihood of success.

Shaping is an excellent strategy for teaching children to respond to simple directions such as coming when their names are called or to improve various sports skills (such as throwing a ball, jumping, running, etc.). For example, if your child does not seem to react when his name is called, you first would find a small reward that he enjoys, one that he immediately tries to take when he sees it. In this situation, while you are standing about 10 feet from your child, you can call out his name, and, even if he does not react in any manner, you would slowly approach him while holding his special toy in your open hand. At some point while you are approaching him, he is likely to see the toy and reach for it. Sometime later (when you have the toy again), you repeat this process and continue to gradually walk toward him. After a few opportunities like this, he is likely to notice you while you are walking toward him. At that point, slow down so that he will start walking to you.

Continue this process of calling and approaching, and you are likely to find that upon calling your child's name, he looks toward you and starts to approach. At this point, after you call his name, gradually begin to hide the toy so that he sees you but not the toy. Once he reaches you, praise him and of course give him the toy. Over time, when he approaches you after you call his name, you can use other reinforcers, especially praise and hugs. Eventually, you may introduce some simple tasks for him to do before providing praise. In this manner, he has learned to come to you when you call his name. Sometimes he gets a material reward, sometimes simple social rewards, and sometimes a small task to perform. Notice you did not prompt him during any part of this lesson. Yes, shaping behavior requires great patience on your part but the outcome is well worth it!

In teaching athletic skills, such as throwing a ball, shaping will be far more effective than trying to find an effective prompt. For example, if your child can toss a ball while you stand 2 feet away, you can then try standing 2½ to 3 feet away and praise all successful throws. Gradually move further away and praise all good throws. If you find that you reach a point where you've stepped too far away—several errors have occurred in a row—then move a bit closer to the point where your child succeeds again. When you have successfully "stretched" the length of your child's throws on one day, you may want to try shortening that distance a bit at the start of the next day while aiming to exceed the previous day's limit by the end of the new day. Many coaches apply this strategy in their training, even if they don't describe it as shaping!

Shaping has been successfully used to teach all types of skills. It can be used to help children articulate more clearly, improve their penmanship, be more creative in terms of artwork and writing, and almost anything you can think of! The keys to using shaping are:

1. to know what your child can currently do,
2. to have precise information on what you want your child to do, and
3. to develop a clear plan to identify tiny steps between those two behaviors.

Shaping takes patience and a keen eye (or ear!). You will be tempted to add prompts in an effort to make the learning process go more quickly, but you must remember that you will have to remove every prompt you add into a lesson. With shaping, there are no prompts to remove!

For more information about how to use the power of shaping in your home (for everyone!), you may want to check out Karen Pryor's website on clicker-training (www.clickertraining.com) or the TAGTeach International website, for information on teaching various sporting skills (www.tagteach.com). Clicker-training is the term used to describe how teachers can use a simple clicker to provide timely feedback for successful performance. The advantage of a clicker is that we can use it immediately and it always sounds the same—unlike our voice, which often varies in tone, quality, strength or some other feature. Clicker-training has even been used successfully to help train high-level gymnastics students.

Video Learning

Video learning (video modeling) is a relatively new teaching method in which peers, siblings, or adults are videotaped performing a skill correctly and then the video is shown repeatedly to a child who needs to learn that skill. A number of recent studies have shown that many children with and without autism can effectively learn skills and routines if they first watch videotaped examples and are then quickly given an opportunity to practice the modeled skills. This strategy has been shown to be effective for teaching both communication and motor skills. Some of the skills taught via video modeling have included play skills such as having a tea party, going shopping, and baking. More advanced social skills, such as perspective-taking, can also be improved via video modeling (Charlop-Christy and Daneshvar, 2003).

Some researchers have shown that having children watch videos of themselves—video self-modeling—can help them learn to more consistently use skills that they only occasionally use. For example, two researchers (Wert and Neisworth, 2003) demonstrated that children learned to be more spontaneous with their spoken requests after watching videos of themselves making requests in guided situations.

Review

In this chapter, we've reviewed some general guidelines that should help you create effective lessons at home and in your community. In teaching most lessons, you will need to help your child perform a task—typically, by using a variety of prompts. Whenever you use a prompt, however, you also need a plan to eliminate that prompt so that your child will be able to perform the task without your assistance, in response to cues that are part of the natural environment, including the social surroundings. There are many strategies for eliminating prompts and none will work in every situation all of the time. Therefore, you should try to vary the types of prompts you use and the types of strategies you use to get rid of those prompts.

It is possible to teach without the use of prompts by using shaping. This strategy relies upon reinforcing small changes in behavior that add up over time to dramatic changes in performance. Although shaping requires patience and attention to detail, it has the advantage of not requiring a strategy to eliminate prompts.

In the next chapter, we will look at strategies used in the Pyramid Approach to minimize the chances that a child will make errors when learning, as well as ways to thoughtfully respond to errors when they do occur.

6 Dealing with Common Errors

Keiko is washing dishes when her son, Yoshi, walks into the room from the bathroom. Keiko hears the faucet still running so she says, "Please go turn off the water." Yoshi does as she asks. The next day, Keiko again hears that Yoshi has not turned the faucet off after he has been to the bathroom. She again reminds him about what he needs to do. After five days in a row of this pattern, Keiko is getting exasperated, wondering why her son cannot learn this simple rule about when to turn off the water. Her husband comments, "But Keiko, he does know when to turn the water off—he does it when you tell him to!"

As we suggested, our preference is to try to teach in ways that limit the likelihood of errors—"trial and success" is a good motto to follow! Still, no matter how tiny may be the steps we design, all children will make mistakes at some point. Sometimes, we'll see the mistake within a formal lesson that we've created, while at other times, we'll notice an error during a time when we're not even conscious of an ongoing lesson taking place. The key to long-term effective learning often is how well we respond to these errors.

On the one hand, adults often feel that it is a good idea just to repeat things if a child makes an error—maybe the child would do better with another chance. However, you might want to follow the advice of a brilliant man who is not often thought of as a teacher. Albert Einstein once said that it is insane to "do the same thing over and over but expect a different outcome." How does this relate to teaching? Well, think of how many times you've repeated yourself (or watched others repeat themselves): "Michelle, come here.... Come here, Michelle . . . come here! Come on, now, come here . . . you can do it . . . come here now . . . COME HERE!" If we ask the child a question or use some type of prompt and the child does not respond correctly, should we repeat the prompt that we just determined was ineffective? Why should we expect a different outcome if we repeat what already hasn't worked? It seems that Einstein would suggest doing something differently after an error, and we would agree. If a prompt doesn't work, try a different way to help.

How should we help? That is easier to figure out if you know the kind of lesson being taught. As Chapter 4 explains, some lessons involve discrete trials and others involve sequences of steps. Because these are two very different types of lessons, we should use two very different types of strategies to handle errors.

Handling Errors During Discrete Trials

Let's say you asked your daughter, Emily, to bring you a cup, but instead she brought you a sock that was lying on the floor. Since she did not seem to understand the spoken word, "cup," repeating it is more likely to result in another error than the correct response. You know that Emily does a good job of getting things when you point to an item. So, rather than repeat your request, you point to the cup. She now brings you the cup. However, you now may well wonder whether Emily is learning the lesson you are trying to teach. After all, this was not a lesson about "bring you things you point to"; rather, it started as a "listen to my instruction" lesson.

We would like to see if Emily really can understand our spoken words. So, we put the cup back, and ask Emily again to bring the cup. This time she does so correctly. But are we done with the lesson? Some of you may have a queasy feeling because you notice that Emily brought you the cup twice in a row. Does she really understand what you are saying or is she just repeating the last successful thing she did (a very good learner-strategy, by the way). So, we provide a little praise and we put the cup back. Now, to make sure that Emily is listening to us (rather than getting locked into her own pattern of repeating the last correct action) we ask her to get something that she already knows how to do—get a ball. Immediately after she brings us the ball (because she always does this task well), we ask for the cup. Now, if she brings the cup, we can feel more confident that she has indeed listened to our request, so we also provide some enthusiastic praise (and fill the cup with something she likes to drink).

These steps may seem complicated and take a little time to adjust to but they will help speed up the learning process and help reduce the chances that the child will get stuck on the type of help you provide (some people call this "prompt dependency"). Notice that this was a discrete trial type of lesson—simple question, simple response. Once the error occurred:

1. We helped in a manner that showed, modeled, or demonstrated the correct answer.
2. We then used the original cue to encourage the child to repeat in a practice fashion—that is, we give some praise, but not a lavish amount, for a correct response.
3. We next switched or changed the task to something that the child is already good at doing (this varies from child to child, and from occasion to occasion). We also used this third step to help assure that the child was really attending to us.
4. Finally, we repeated our original request and provided a nice reward for successful completion of the task.

Not surprisingly, we call this the 4-step Error Correction Procedure to help us remember each of the four steps that leads to improved learning. Refer to Table 6-1 on the next page for a description of this error correction strategy for one lesson.

You may find opportunities for this type of error-correction strategy even when you are not conducting a formal lesson. For example, your daughter is helping you load the washing machine and you have a pile of clothes that has both dark and light pieces. Your aim is to load only the "whites" for this load. As you load the laundry, your daughter reaches for an item that is "dark." You can gently block this error and immediately point to a light item (model) and gesture (practice) for your child to put that one in the machine without providing much praise. Then you could ask her for a clothespin (something that she knows very well)—this would be your "switch" step. Next you would gesture (repeat) to the pile (without pointing to any one piece) and when she takes out a light piece, praise her generously! This 4-step

Table 6-1 | Using the 4-Step Error Correction Sequence

Step name	Teacher action	Child action
	"Give me the apple"	Gives an orange
1. Model	Points to and taps on apple	Gives the apple
	Replaces apple	
2 . Practice	"Give me the apple"	Gives the apple
	Quietly says, "Good"	
3. Switch/change	"Where's Mickey?"	Points to Mickey Mouse doll
	Quietly says, "That's right"	
4. Repeat	"Give me the apple"	Gives the apple
	"That's great!" and hands over a cut piece to eat	

error correction can be used whenever a task involves discrete trials, whether or not you are setting up a true lesson or just reacting within a naturally occurring opportunity.

There may be times when your child repeats the error at the last step of your correction sequence. In this case you may repeat the entire four steps. However, too many repetitions of the error will likely lead to an emotional outburst and little learning, so we advise running through the 4-step sequence two or three times at most before ending the situation (on a positive note if possible—after a successful switch, for example). At that point, you should move on to something else while you think about what went wrong. Perhaps your child is too tired or bored or simply not motivated to learn your lesson at that point.

Handling Errors during Sequential Lessons

Backstepping

Remember, not all lessons involve discrete trials. Many lessons involve sequential tasks. What should you do when your child makes errors in this type of lesson—either errors of omission—she pauses or simply doesn't do a step, or errors of commission—she does the wrong thing at a certain step?

Let's suppose you're baking a batch of pre-mix cookies. Part of the sequence calls for the child to turn on the oven, set the temperature, put the dough on the tray, open the oven, insert the tray of cookies, close the oven door, and set the timer. As you watch your daughter, you see that she has put the tray in the oven but did not start the oven or set the temperature. You know that if you now point to the correct buttons, she will start the oven and also set the temperature. This approach will fix the immediate problem but will it lead to improved learning? That is, what do you think she will do the next time she bakes cookies? Right—she will put the tray in and wait for you to remind her to push the correct buttons.

How should we handle this type of error within a sequence? We think it is important to understand that each step should act as the signal for the next step. Putting in the tray should only follow starting the oven and setting the temperature and putting the dough on the tray. If we help outside of the proper sequence, we will maintain that inappropriate sequence. Therefore, we need to recreate the correct sequence. In this case, we would calmly tell the child to try it again and take the tray out of the oven and put it back on the kitchen counter (because putting the dough on the tray was the last successful step). Then we would prompt her to start the oven and to set the temperature before getting her to put the tray in the oven. This strategy seeks to link setting the temperature to finishing putting the dough on the tray. Thus, we have stepped back into the sequence just before the error took place. We call this type of error correction backstepping. You can review the use of backstepping in Table 6-2 on the next page.

Now, we realize that it is far simpler to just point to the temperature button on the oven and thus fix the problem. But fixing the problem now may not lead to avoiding the problem in the future. Only if the child learns the proper sequence will she be able to perform the steps in their proper order the next time. So, it will be worthwhile to spend a little extra time on this occasion in order to save a lot of time down the road when you would keep having to remind your child to set the temperature.

Let's look at another example of using backstepping. What would you do if your child slammed the door too hard upon entering your car? You might be tempted to tell your child not to do that again or to

Table 6-2 | Using Backstep Error Correction with Hand-washing Routine

Correct sequence	Actual sequence	Teacher Backstep actions
1. Pick up soap	Picks up soap	
2. Turn on water	Turns on water	
3. Wet hands/soap	Wets hands/soap	
4. Put soap down	Puts soap down	
5. Rub hands	Rubs hands	
6. Rinse hands	Rinses hands	
7. Turn water off		
8. Dry hands	Dries hands	
9. Leave bathroom	Leaves bathroom	1. Take child back into bathroom (no scolding!)
		2. Help child get hands wet and soapy
		3. When child rinses hands, prompt to turn off water
		4. Allow to dry hands
		5. Praise and reward for completing routine!

tell her to open and close the door gently while she is sitting in the car. However, using the backstep error correction strategy, you would ask your child to get out of the car and reenter it while guiding her to gently close the door. This way you help her associate entering the car with proper handling of the door, not merely following your instructions.

If your child refuses to go back within the sequence, you should check on a couple of things. First, make sure that your tone of voice is not harsh or punitive. It should be matter-of-fact and supportive, as in, "Let's try that again!" You should also check and determine whether your child is motivated to complete the activity. If she is not motivated to complete the task, then you will need to address this issue before modifying your teaching strategy. Finally, if the situation itself is difficult to replicate, you may consider the strategy described in the next section.

Anticipatory Prompts

There will be occasions when you will find it hard to arrange for an immediate backstep. Some tasks at home and in the community will not permit any type of restart. For example, think about helping your child to put the right amount of liquid soap into the dishwasher dispenser. If she makes a mistake and pours in a quarter-cup too much, would you want to back-step then, have her put in the correct amount, and then turn on the machine? Only if you are prepared to work on mopping up the extra suds!

Or, perhaps you are at a movie theater, and, after standing in a long line for a popular movie, your son has walked past the ticket collector without giving him the ticket. If you wanted to use the backstep strategy you would need to get back in the line so that your son can associate approaching the ticket collector with giving the ticket. Of course, that is very impractical in this situation. We suggest that you will need to anticipate this error during the next natural opportunity (or during a mock-movie-ticket rehearsal in some other locale) and give your son some help before he once again makes the error that you can anticipate.

This type of anticipatory prompt is helpful when you know that an error is likely to occur. Thus, as you approach the end of the line, you could use a direct reminder: "Hold out your ticket for the collector" or a more indirect prompt, "Remember what to do with your ticket" or "What will you do with your ticket?" You will know if you have an effective prompt if your child hands over the ticket at the right time! Likewise, when it comes to measuring out soap for the dishwasher, you would need to provide an effective prompt—perhaps a bright red line on the cup at the correct level—prior to the next opportunity to load the dishes.

Sometimes you may realize that your child has made an error but you have no time to run through an error correction sequence. For example, your sixteen-year-old needs to leave the house in the next two minutes to catch the school bus and you realize she has not put on her deodorant. In this type of situation, we would suggest that you simply take care of the immediate problem (fix it!) and save your error-correction for the next occasion. If we don't have time to teach, then we still should take care of our children. That is, immediately help your child apply deodorant on this occasion but be sure to use an anticipatory prompt tomorrow!

Review

Our first goal as teachers is to promote learning with as few errors as possible. In this manner we try to assure that learning is a positive experience for our children. When errors do occur, we should understand the type of lesson we are teaching before deciding how to respond to the error. We can view errors as an opportunity to practice the correct response. Errors made within discrete types of lessons can lead to the use of a 4-step error correction sequence as a way to help the child perform without an immediate prompt. Within sequential lessons, we should focus on linking each step in the correct order. Consequently, we may need to backstep to assure that the chain is being constructed in the correct manner. When going back to an earlier part of a sequence is not possible or practical, then we can anticipate that the error will take place similarly on the next opportunity and provide some type of prompt to prevent the repetition of that particular error. Remember, don't simply fix the problem—teach a skill via error correction!

In the next chapter, we will take a look at another issue that may be problematic within your family—what to do when your child doesn't act his or her best!

7 Dealing with Difficult Behaviors

After a long day at the office, Mary comes home and asks Bob how the day went with their son, Vince. Bob immediately tells her that Vince pinched his arm several times and points to the new dent in the wall that Vince made when he threw a chair. He asks Mary if she knows what they can do to get Vince to stop these outbursts. She asks Bob if he knows why Vince is doing these things and he admits that he's not sure. Mary and Bob realize that it will be hard to plan for a change without better understanding their son's actions.

Context and Magnitude

All children, including those with autism spectrum disorders, at least occasionally engage in actions that we adults are not happy to witness. In general, there are a host of behaviors that we wish would either disappear, or, at a minimum, would decrease in severity or frequency. Part of the difficulty parents face in determining which problem behaviors to address is deciding which behaviors are truly problematic. We may feel that certain behaviors are always inappropriate, but a more careful review of this issue reveals that the setting for an action may influence how we view that action.

For example, we observe a young boy shouting loudly. If he were screaming in his home kitchen, then we might feel confident that this behavior is not appropriate. However, if the boy is at a baseball game and is rooting for his brother's team, then shouting support may be perfectly acceptable—and even encouraged. Similarly, slapping my own face may be inappropriate—unless I am trying to stop a mosquito from biting me. In other words, the setting—or context—will influence how we view a behavior. To remind us of this issue, we will refer to *contextually inappropriate behaviors* (*CIBs*) when we are dealing with actions that we hope to reduce or eliminate.

Just as we consider context of a behavior, we must also consider issues associated with the frequency or intensity of an action. Asking people how they are feeling is an appropriate skill, but asking the question every minute for an entire hour is not appropriate. Knocking on a door to see if someone is home is fine, but punching your fist through the windowpane is not reasonable.

We must also consider the severity of the problematic behavior. If you simply watch someone else over a length of time, it is highly likely that you will notice some little actions that you wouldn't do or that even bother you to watch. For example, why does she play with her hair? Why does he tap on the tabletop? Why does she have to double knot her shoelaces? While these actions may be irritating, they really do not rise to the level of concern that you must work hard to eliminate them.

Behaviors that we want to eliminate include:

- actions that are harmful to the child (i.e., self-injury), to other people (i.e., aggression), or to the environment (tantrums, property destruction, etc.);
- actions that significantly interfere with routine activities (e.g., self-stimulation, disruptive noise, etc.), either for the child or for others; or
- actions that may bring social sanctions against the child or caretakers (e.g., disrobing in public, speaking in a weird or bizarre manner, certain lengthy rituals, etc.).

It is important to note that the mere presence of self-stimulatory actions is not a sufficient justification to seek to eliminate that behavior. Self-stimulatory behaviors may include odd actions such as flicking fingers and hopping on toes but they also include rather common actions such as twirling hair and chewing gum. In fact, everyone engages in self-stimulatory behaviors, and it is likely impossible to eliminate all of them. Instead, we should focus on the impact that such actions have on other important behavior. That is, if Hank rocks his foot under the table but pays complete attention to everything happening around him, then his foot rocking does not need to be addressed. On the other hand, if he flicks his fingers before his eyes and does not pay attention when his name is called or other important things are said to him, then finger play poses a serious problem and should be addressed.

Why Did He Do That?

Once your family has decided that something your child does needs to be addressed, several key factors must be considered. Now that you have your focal point—your "target behavior"—you will need to act as a news reporter and determine: Why is this happening? What can we do about it? How can we make a change? Do we have the resources to make this change? And finally, was this a good change?

Let's consider Rosalie's situation. Her daughter, Natalie, often screams while they are shopping in the local mall. First, Rosalie must consider why this may be happening. To simplify the possibilities, we will consider three main factors. One, Natalie may be screaming in order to *gain something*—possibly her mother's attention or something material. Perhaps in the past, when Natalie screamed, Rosalie bought her some candy to calm her down. In this case, Natalie has learned that the best way to get candy is to scream. Another broad possibility is that Natalie is trying to *avoid* or *escape* something. For example, maybe Rosalie leaves the mall whenever Natalie screams and that is precisely what Natalie wants—to get out of the noisy, crowded situation. The final general possibility we will consider is that Natalie's screams are *elicited* in a manner similar to reflexes. These actions are somewhat different than actions that reliably lead to a predictable outcome and are often thought of as "emotionally driven." Think about not only how you feel but also the often useless behaviors you engage in while waiting for an elevator to arrive or when you've just been told that the baseball or football game you've been waiting to watch has been cancelled due to rain. You might even scream at the TV, knowing full well that this will not help the situation. Similarly, Natalie may scream because she is frustrated over waiting to get to her favorite store, or because her shoes are too tight and hurt.

Why is it important to figure out what is leading to the contextually inappropriate behavior (CIB)? Let's assume that Natalie is screaming because she wants candy. Now, suppose that we magically eliminate her screaming. What does she still want? Right, she still wants candy and may not have calm communication skills that would help her get candy when she wants it. So, even if we could magically get rid of her screaming, she now will have to figure out some other way to get candy while at the mall. And it is not likely that her next solution to this problem will be more pleasant. Furthermore, her mother doesn't think that having candy is a bad thing for Natalie—it is the screaming that she doesn't like.

Similarly, if Natalie were screaming to leave the mall, even if we could magically get her to stop screaming, she would still want to leave and may not have another calm way of indicating that to her mother. Finally, if she is screaming because she is frustrated about how long it is taking to get to her favorite store, then her mother must either rearrange her shopping schedule or teach Natalie to improve her ability to wait for things she likes.

In each scenario, Rosalie must first determine what is leading Natalie to scream in order to determine the best course of action.

To summarize, ***functions of behavior*** are often categorized as:

1. to obtain a desired object or activity, including social outcomes;
2. to escape or avoid someone or something;
3. elicited by the properties of the situation.

We cannot go into great detail here about how you determine what function is controlling your child's behavior. Briefly, you need to not only monitor the behavior itself but also important factors that occur both before (e.g., location, time, activity, people present, and other types of relevant stimuli) and after the behavior (e.g., consequences introduced or removed, both social and materials). It may be helpful to try to guess at which of the three key functions the behavior seems to be serving for your child on each occasion it occurs and see if there is a pattern over time. For more information on determining the purpose of your child's behavior, you may want to read *Functional Behavior Assessment for People with Autism* by Beth Glasberg.

Choosing a Replacement Behavior

The best course of action will not focus just on eliminating the problematic behavior, because that leaves the root cause in place. We must also focus on teaching the child a more appropriate way to meet

his or her goal. For example, Natalie's mother will have to help Natalie learn a more appropriate way to achieve her own goal—whether it is to get something she likes, such as candy; to get away from something she doesn't like, such as the noise level; or to improve her ability to wait for things she likes, and thus improve her emotional responding. Unless Natalie learns these replacement skills, when the old needs arise, she will likely revert to her old ways or try something else that her mother will not be pleased to witness.

Notice that the potential replacement behaviors for Natalie involve those critical functional communication skills that we stressed teaching and supporting earlier in this book. In general, we advocate teaching functional communication skills as early and as strongly as possible. This way, when CIBs do arise, their potential alternatives are skills that the child has already acquired. If your child has not learned the replacement skill for a particular CIB, then you will have to spend time on developing that skill, as opposed to more simply making sure your child uses the skill.

Another important point—although some replacement skills involve expressive communication, such as asking for a favorite item, a break, or help, other replacement skills involve receptive skills, such as learning to wait. Simply being able to express needs, such as, "I want to go to the music store *now*!" or even pointing out the problem, such as, "I'm getting upset that it's taking so long to get to the music store!" may not solve the problem. That is, no matter what your child is able to express, getting to the music store will take some time.

There are several things you'll want to consider when selecting replacement behaviors. For example, it is easier to pick a replacement that your child can already do as opposed to needing to teach a new skill. The replacement should be relatively easy and efficient to perform so that there is no natural preference for the original behavior. Of course, the replacement also should be one that is socially acceptable.

If waiting is the issue, then remember to plan for something that your child can do while waiting for the main goal. Rosalie needs to consider what Natalie can do while waiting to get to the music store. She should not expect her daughter to simply not get upset. That would be a hard goal for anyone. Depending on Natalie's skill level, Rosalie might ask her to try to find five people with red hair, or find the letter "Q" in five store signs, or simply talk to her about what happened at school that day. What Natalie is asked to do while waiting should be relatively easy—not a new or difficult skill—just something to help pass the time.

It is also important to support replacement skills that truly meet the child's needs, rather than being something that you want to see instead. For example, while Mandy is watching TV at home, her son, Frank, frequently runs around the room, often knocking things over and making a mess. Mandy would prefer that he sit in a chair while she watches her TV show. She knows that he likes licorice so she tries to make a deal—if he sits, she'll give him some licorice.

Although this type of arrangement may work for a short time, Mandy has not determined why her son was running around in the first place. It is very unlikely that Frank has been running around to get licorice. It is more likely that other factors are at play. He may run around to get her attention. And even though he likes licorice, when he really wants her attention, he will run once more. He may be running because he does not like her show and he is trying to get her to turn it off. He may be running because he is bored and frustrated that, from his point of view, nothing worthwhile will happen until after the TV show. Therefore, Mandy cannot just pick a replacement behavior for her son and an arbitrary reward for that behavior, but must figure out why Frank is running around before she tries to intervene and help him to change his ways.

Determining the function of the CIB and the best possible replacement that will meet the same needs may require the assistance of a specialist— especially if the behavior is particularly dangerous. The field of applied behavior analysis (ABA) provides training and support to help families and schools make this type of determination in complex cases. The Association for Behavior Analysis International (www.abainternational.org) has a Special Interest Group (SIG) for autism and this group can help families find competent specialists to help in this endeavor.

Whether or not you consult with a specialist in behavior analysis in selecting a replacement behavior, your family should involve your child's school (or other program). You and the school staff need to coordinate what you are doing since it can be confusing to children to have to cope with different rules in different situations.

Once you have selected a replacement behavior, you also will need to implement a plan to assure that this replacement meets with success. That is, you must plan to reward your child when he use the replacement behavior, and even encourage him to practice the particular skill when the CIB is not occurring, to be certain that it is well developed and readily used. In Chapter 2, we described several ways of "catching them being good." Use these strategies whenever you are trying to improve the likelihood that your child will use the replacement skill instead of the CIB. Remember, if you do not adequately reward your child for the replacement skill, then he will use whatever CIB has been effective.

In general, **the key to long-term successful intervention with contextually inappropriate behaviors** rests with:

1. identifying the function of the behavior, and
2. systematically replacing it with a socially appropriate and functionally comparable alternative.

If a child screams to get attention, he can be taught to communicate via words, pictures, or signs that he wants someone to interact with him. If a child is hitting his head because he sees a toy that is out of reach, he can be taught to communicate to request the toy directly or to ask for help to get to the toy. If a child slaps his face when the toy he is playing with stops working, he can be taught to communicate to ask for help. If a child is putting his head down on the dining room table midway through setting the table, he can be taught to ask for a brief break. And if a child is punching the wall when he is told he cannot go outside to play right now, he can be taught how to wait for gradually longer and longer periods of time. In each of these examples, the solution—including choosing the replacement behavior—depends upon understanding why the target behavior is occurring.

Altering the Environment vs. Teaching Replacement Behaviors

Many people try to avoid situations that provoke the problem behavior. For example, if the child with autism does not like noisy or visually stimulating environments, then they avoid going into such settings. Some families and schools have their children work long hours alone in cubicles that visually block the typical stimulation of classrooms or rooms within the house. While these types of strategies will lead to fewer behavior problems, they will not teach the child how to cope with noisy or stimulating environments when they are unavoidable.

Sometimes a better strategy to help the child pay attention to critical parts of the environment is to increase the motivation (positive outcomes) for paying attention. Let's examine a fairly common experience for adults before we think of applying this strategy for our children. Imagine that you are at a noisy party talking to someone who is rather boring. Most likely, you are having problems hearing that person talk because of the surrounding (and distracting) noise. Suddenly, the person you've been waiting to talk to comes over and starts a conversation—the very thing you've been hoping for! Do you now have any trouble hearing what is being said to you? Of course not. And not because the room really became quieter but because it is now much more rewarding to hear what is being said to you. In the same manner, rather than always trying to turn down the noise of the room for your child, you may want to design a system that strongly rewards him for paying attention and doing whatever it is that you are aiming for. These aims can include substituting replacement behaviors for those unwanted CIBs.

For example, your child may be able to set the table when only the two of you are in the room but you want to improve his ability to complete the task in the face of distractions. We'll also assume that you've successfully used a token system to reward your child when he has successfully set the table. Once your child begins to set the table, ask someone else in your home to come into the room and begin talking to you. As long as your child continues to set the table, give him tokens. If he stops setting the table, remind him about what he is working for—the reward you've set up. Once he is able to set the table in this circumstance, gradually add other distractions—other people coming into the kitchen, turning on the radio or TV, turning on noisy appliances like the dishwasher or a blender, and other similarly distracting but natural events. Notice that you should not introduce all of these at once but rather teach your child to pay attention by gradually increasing distractions while continuing to use the powerful reward system.

We are not saying that you should never try to reduce annoying circumstances. For example, many people use noise-attenuating headphones on airplanes and in other noisy environments, and those with autism can well adopt these same strategies. Our main point is to try to prepare the child for situations in which the headset doesn't work, or when being in a noisy, visually distracting situation is unavoidable, without the child having to resort to a CIB.

Should We Use Punishment?

As noted, the most important aspect of any behavior intervention package is identifying why the contextually inappropriate behavior is occurring and then implementing a plan to assure the child will use a better replacement behavior. Preventive and ameliorative strategies also will be helpful. Still, even with the best of prevention and replacement strategies, we should recognize that if a child has frequently spat at people for the past several years, it is highly likely that another spitting episode will occur before significant progress is seen.

Ignoring Behavior

What, then, should parents and others do when the contextually inappropriate behavior does take place? Many people automatically think, "Ignore it!" This strategy may be helpful if the CIB is motivated by some type of reward that you can eliminate. However, if the CIB is related to your child's desire for escape or avoidance, ignoring him may be precisely what he wants! So, we first must understand that how we react should be related to why the behavior is taking place.

If the CIB is related to getting attention, then ignoring the child should be helpful. Of course, ignoring screams or tantrums is not easy! Rather than simply trying not to respond, you may do better if you plan something specific that results in the equivalent of not attending to your child. For example, one parent took out a specific notebook and began to write her thoughts (including angry ones!) while her child was screaming at her. Because she was intent on her writing, she did not pay attention to the screaming. Another parent put on a headset and listened to classical music whenever her son took all the pots and pans out from the cabinet. Again, she engaged in something that helped her not attend to the noise of the crashing pots and pans.

If you decide to try to use ignoring (more formally called *extinction*), you must be certain that you can follow through on your plan. To make this happen, you must be able to assure that your child will only receive the reward connected to the CIB with your permission. For example, if you are trying to withhold attention for screaming but you know that your other children will likely provide some attention, then your strategy of ignoring the behavior will not truly be implemented. If you cannot completely control the reward for your child's CIB, then you risk rewarding the CIB after your child has escalated his efforts, essentially making the reduction or elimination of the CIB more difficult. If the potential reward—social attention, for example—can be provided by more than one person—every adult in the home, in this case—then everyone must use the strategy or it will not be effective for anyone.

Time Out

Another commonly used strategy is time out (TO). This strategy works best when the CIB is associated with receiving some type of reward and may be helpful in situations involving elicited actions. For example, if your child starts to scream because he wants you to take him outside or because he simply wants you to play with him, time out can be part of an effective strategy. It is not as likely to be effective for escape- or avoidance-related behaviors. If your child is smiling on the way to the TO area, then you are not using the right intervention!

To implement time out in your home, you will most likely want to designate a specific location that is boring (*not* the child's room), but not scary (*not* a small, closed closet). When you observe your child engaging in the CIB, calmly and matter-of-factly tell him to go to time out. Most likely, you will have to firmly guide your child to the area, where you may have placed a chair. Have a kitchen-timer (or similar device) by the chair and set it for one to two minutes. Setting the timer for longer periods of time has not been shown to be more effective and reduces the child's opportunities to learn appropriate alternatives.

While your child is in the TO area, try not to interact in any manner—no eye contact or facial reactions to anything your child does (short of seriously hurting himself). If he attempts to leave, firmly and physically guide him to stay in the chair but try to do this without talking or explaining what you are doing. When the timer rings, announce the end of TO and immediately point out what reward your child can earn for some appropriate action—the same rewards you had made available before you started the activity. This last step is crucial: time-***out*** works only if time-***in*** is rewarding. From your child's point of view, if there are no benefits to being out of TO, then why bother to leave?

You can use TO in the community, although implementing it away from your home can be a little trickier. If you routinely go to a park, then pick a spot that will serve as the TO area—somewhere that you can reasonably assure the other children will not play with your child. If you visit someone else's home, pick a location as soon as you arrive—even the bottom of a staircase may serve the purpose. If you are in a community setting such as a store or the mall, then you may want to use a ribbon or light necklace to signal time out. That is, if your child engages in a problem behavior, place the ribbon or necklace around your child's neck and set a timer.

During the timed period, try to ignore everything your child does. Your child may well escalate his inappropriate behavior, but as long as it is not dangerous to him or others or particularly destructive, it is best to continue to ignore his attempts to force interactions with you. Once the timer rings, signal the end of TO by reminding your child about the potential rewards for appropriate actions—for example, going to his favorite store for calmly walking with you, picking out a piece of candy for holding onto the box of cereal while in the supermarket, etc. Remind others with you about the rule associated with wearing the ribbon.

Verbal Reprimands

When your child is engaging in a problem behavior, you also may want to say, "No" or "Stop," or use some other type of quick verbal reprimand. Your child is very likely to hear these words at school or in the community, so it is a good idea to teach him what they mean. There are a few simple rules for using verbal reprimands:

1. Use a matter-of-fact tone of voice and speak loudly enough that you are sure that you've been heard. Screaming, yelling, or shouting will not make the message more effective and may generate reactions that will be counterproductive.

2. Avoid using a singsong manner: “no, no, no!!” This style will diminish the serious intent of the message.

You may want to teach your child what “no” and “stop” mean in situations when everyone is calm and the likelihood of any CIB is remote. For example, you may set up a game in which your child is searching through various closed boxes for a treat or favorite toy. You calmly say, “no” as your child approaches an empty box and immediately encourage him to try another box. In this manner, “no” comes to provide useful information to your child as well as informing him not to proceed with an action.

Similarly, you may set up a game of tag, or some equivalent game involving chasing. It is important to try this game in a safe situation—a hallway or room where the exits are already secured. When you say, “run,” you will chase your child when he runs and make the chase exciting. When you say, “stop,” the rule is that if your child stops, you will walk over and then restart the game. However, if your child does not stop, then you end the game (possibly by just walking away). This type of game teaches your child the value of responding to “stop” in a safe setting before you need to try it in a more difficult situation.

Fines

If you are using a type of token or other visual reward system (e.g., collecting puzzle pieces or letters that spell out the name of the reward) you will be tempted to use fines if your child behaves inappropriately. We advise that you not take away tokens that your child has already earned by good learning or other positive actions. Instead, you may want to create a separate system that builds in a type of countdown strategy. For example, your daughter may enjoy playing on the computer but she also has a rude habit of yelling to get your attention. You give her a card that has five pictures of the computer game she likes to play. You also remind her to use her “inside voice” when she begins to speak to you. Of course, you will reward her with attention whenever she uses an appropriate tone. But when she does yell, you remind her of what she should do (speak quietly) and remove one of the pictures.

After an hour (or whatever your goal is), if she has at least one computer picture remaining, then give her access to her favorite game for some time. This way, you can have a deal in place for good "work"(your token system related to the learning goals you have established for her) and a separate deal for good "behavior" (your count-down system connected with the computer).

Don't Forget to Evaluate What You're Doing!

Let's be realistic. Although you probably know it is important to evaluate the strategies you are using, it is not easy to do so while you are dealing with an inappropriate behavior. However, we want to stress the importance of this type of evaluation. We should never scold, reprimand, ignore, or use time out if it is not producing the outcome we are hoping for—reducing or eliminating a contextually inappropriate behavior. Therefore, if you are willing to put in the time and effort to use some type of intervention, then you also must be willing to put in time and effort to collect information to assure its success. How you collect information may depend upon what it is you are trying to modify. In Chapter 8, we will describe ways that you can collect this type of information at home and in the community.

We know that data collection and evaluation can seem like a daunting task, but we also are sure that significantly reducing your child's inappropriate behavior is important to you and your family. You may want to set up some type of reward for yourself and the entire family for your successes—that is, remember to treat yourself (and anyone who has been helpful) well! Changing CIBs requires a lot of planning and dedication, so take time to celebrate when things are going well.

Review

Within this area of the Pyramid Approach, we've talked about many aspects of dealing with contextually inappropriate behaviors. First, you must determine why the behavior is taking place. Next, you must identify a replacement behavior that is directly related to what you've figured out in the first step. Then, you need a system to assure that the replacement will be effective in getting your child what he wants and that he will be rewarded for using the new behavior. Next, you need to measure changes in the CIB and the potential replacement behavior, and then decide whether the change is appropriate or whether you need to modify your strategy. Finally, if things have improved, enjoy the fruits of your labor!

The next critical area of the Pyramid Approach addresses how to best evaluate whether our teaching and behavior intervention plans are truly effective.

8 Evaluating What You Are Doing

Amanda comes home and watches her husband, Scott, setting the table with their daughter, Amy. She asks Scott how things are going. He says, "Well, sometimes I think she's got it and other times it seems that she's never seen a fork in her life!" They both have been working with Amy on this task for several months and wonder whether they should just give up and set the table themselves.

Peter and Beth have been trying to help their son, Tony, decrease the amount of time he spends humming very loudly. They've put time into determining why Tony seems to do this, and they think they've developed a good intervention plan. And yet, some days Tony seems content to quietly listen to music but on other days he hums as long and as loudly as ever. They don't see an easy pattern so they are not sure what to do next.

We all hope that the skills our children learn will make a big difference in our lives. Many of us also think that these changes will be readily noticed—for example, my daughter couldn't talk but now she does; my son couldn't tie his shoes, but now he can; we used to have to cut up his steak but now he uses a knife and fork with ease. Unfortunately, these positive changes usually do not show up suddenly in a type of "ah-ha!" phenomenon. Instead, most skills are learned gradually and via the accumulation of small improvements over time. We have watched teachers who were actually making progress with their students but didn't realize that they were and were therefore ready to make changes to an effective strategy. On the other hand, we have also observed teachers fail to make changes within ineffective lessons because they did not realize that their students were not making any progress.

We encourage parents to put in time and energy to figure out whether their teaching efforts are worthwhile. If you do not assess what you are doing, then you could be wasting not only your own time but also your child's. How can parents collect information that will help them make good decisions about how to proceed with a lesson or a behavior intervention strategy?

Why Bother to Collect Data?

One of the most important reasons to collect information about your child's performance is to help you answer the question, "Is this a good lesson?" If the answer is "yes," then you should continue to use your strategy. If the answer is "no," and you've given yourself adequate time to make that judgment, then you'll need to change your teaching strategy. The same rationale holds true for intervention plans for contextually inappropriate behavior (CIB).

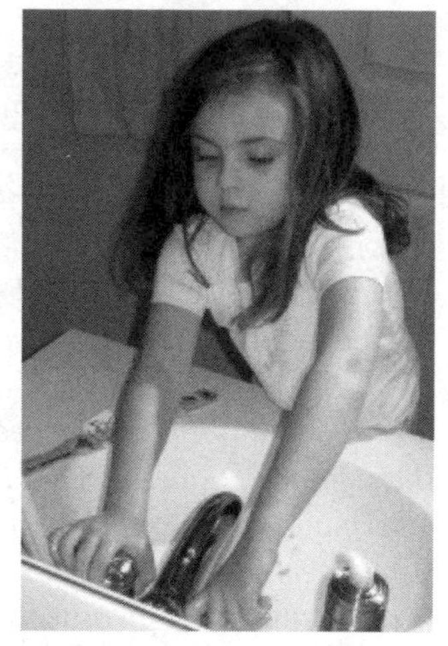

Another reason to take data is that the changes in your child's skills may be subtle. If you don't look carefully for the change, you may miss the improving trend. Not only can you miss the improvement in your child, you may then miss the opportunity to congratulate yourself on a job well done as a teacher! Furthermore, gathering systematic information that shows slow but steady progress can help motivate you to continue with all the hard work it takes to design and implement an effective lesson.

What Type of Information Should We Collect?

Just as there are different skills to learn, different reward systems to use, and different teaching strategies to try, so too are there different targets to gather information about. At times, you may be satisfied with a very general question such as "Are things getting better?" Your medical doctor often starts with this type of question—are you feeling better? If you say "yes," the conversation may well end there. It is when you say "no" that more questions will be asked.

You likely have seen questionnaires that try to set general guidelines about your feelings or sense of what's happening. For example, you might be asked to indicate how much you enjoyed watching a particular movie on a five-point scale—with a one meaning "hated it" and a five meaning "loved it." You may construct a similar type of questionnaire about the skill you are working on with your child, to be completed by each family member once a month (or as often as you think appropriate). For example, if you are trying to improve your child's expressive language skills, the questions may include:

How often did Hannah initiate communicative exchanges this week?

a. 0 to 10 times
b. 11-20 times
c. 20-50 times
d. more than 50 times

How relaxed did Hannah appear while she was talking with her siblings?

a. very anxious
b. somewhat anxious
c. no reaction
d. somewhat happy
e. very happy

How satisfied are you with Hannah's communication skills?

a. very dissatisfied
b. a little disappointed
c. no reaction
d. somewhat happy
e. elated

Notice that you can include a range of specific numbers or you can use a range of general ratings. Furthermore, you can address more advanced or complex skill sets. For example, you can ask:

How independent is Alex in completing the yard work?

a. Needs many spoken reminders (such as "check the mower gas level")
b. Needs some spoken reminders
c. Needs written checklist
d. Sometimes checks written list
e. Does everything independently

What Can/Should You Measure?

As you read these examples, you may feel that there is a very large degree of subjective evaluation included in the process. Your ratings may change because you weren't feeling well that week, or perhaps something especially good happened to you and this helped put a rosy sheen on everything. That is why it may be more effective to develop assessment strategies that can provide precise and unbiased information.

What can you directly measure? Recall that we noted in the Introduction that a learner must "show what she knows." There are many ways that someone can "show" you what she knows, as discussed in the sections below.

Keeping Track of Frequency

You can count how many times something happens—such as how often a child asks for help, or how many times she screamed to-day. Counting occurrences is called taking a *frequency count*. To take a frequency count, you choose the length of time during which you will count a behavior. This will enable you to determine the *rate*, which is the frequency divided by the amount of time you use. For example, you may want to track how often your child asks for help during the morning. If you count 5 occurrences between 9:00 and 11:30, the rate is 2 per hour. You may want to compare that rate with what happens at another time of the day, such as in the evening. If the rate is very different then—perhaps only 0.5 per hour—then you would want to determine why your child appears more independent in the evening than the morning.

Figuring out the rate is very important in situations in which the time intervals are not equal. For example, you should not compare how often your child asked for help during the week with how often she asked for help on the weekend since the time intervals are not the same. You can, however, compare the rates during the two different time periods.

Keeping Track of Intensity

You may be concerned about some feature or characteristic of an action, such as its *intensity*. Perhaps your daughter asks for help but most of the time she says it in a whisper so that it is very hard for anyone to understand her. Counting how often she asks for help will not provide the right information if your goal is to increase how loudly she speaks when asking for help. Or, perhaps your child can say, "No thank you" but screams it at the top of her lungs! The issue is not what she is saying but how she is saying it. In this case, you can measure intensity by devising a rating system in which 1 equals "inaudible," 2 stands for "barely audible," up to a 5 for "much too loud."

Measuring Duration

You may be concerned about how long a particular behavior lasts—its *duration*. For example, you may realize that all three-year-olds have tantrums now and then but you are concerned that your child's tantrums last for 45 minutes or more. A reasonable goal may involve reducing how long the tantrum lasts once it is started. In this case, you are not aiming to immediately eliminate all tantrums, because that is unrealistic. It is reasonable, however, to see if you can help your child decrease the length of her tantrums to five or so minutes.

It also makes sense to measure duration if you are teaching your child to complete a task more quickly. Perhaps Stephanie is teaching her son, Adam, to clean his room. He has learned to put away all of his toys accurately but Stephanie would like him to finish cleaning his room within 15 minutes of when she leaves his room. Currently, it takes him from one-half to a full hour to finish this task.

In this situation, it will be helpful for Stephanie to be very accurate about the duration it takes Adam to clean up. She may set a timer and also let Adam know that if he finishes before the timer rings, then he can play his favorite video game on the large screen TV. At first, she sets an easy goal—50 minutes—because she knows that he usually finishes within this limit. When he is successful at that level for several days, she resets the timer for five fewer minutes. This strategy will only work if

Stephanie accurately records how long it takes to clean the room. There are other specific goals that Stephanie can set, such as how many toys he is able to put back where they belong. In other words, Stephanie's goal will help define what she wants to count.

Measuring Accuracy

Perhaps your child makes a valiant attempt to clean up the playroom but she places the toys almost randomly around the room. That is, there is very little *accuracy* connected with where she puts the toys. You would like to see the balls go in the ball-bin, the stuffed animals in another box, and the train set on its own special shelf. In this case, you don't need to measure how quickly your child cleans up but rather how many things are properly put away. Similarly, perhaps your teenaged son enjoys helping in your workroom but frequently puts the tools in the wrong location, thus making it harder for you to find things when you need them. It's great that he's willing to help but because his accuracy of placement is so poor, it is not really saving you any time.

Writing Goals That Let You Measure the Progress You Are Looking For

As we noted in Chapter 2, you will know you have written a good definition of a goal if two or more people can agree that they are observing the same action, and if your definition makes it clear how you can directly measure whether the goal has been accomplished. However, as explained above, there are different ways to measure progress. When you are writing your goals, you need to be sure to address the aspects of a behavior where you want to see progress. At times, how often something happens—its frequency—can be very important. For example, how many times did your son initiate a request for help? At other times, you may want to measure the rate of an action—as when you determine how many plates your child can put away within 10 minutes after dinner is completed. Sometimes, you will focus on the accuracy of a skill—as when you monitor whether your child puts the plates with the plates and the bowls with the bowls. In some cases, you will be most interested in the duration of an action—as when you time how long your child can play independently while you are doing some housework.

There is no one best way to measure all behaviors. You will need to consider what is most important about an action each time you decide to teach a skill. See Table 8-1 for examples of different types of data to collect.

Table 8-1 | Types of Data Regarding Different Skills & CIBs

Skill	Your Goal	Type of Data
Sorting silverware	Correctly sorts spoons, knives, forks	*Accuracy*
	Empties dishwasher utensil tray in a reasonable amount of time	*Rate*
Interactions with older sisters	Asks sisters for toy	*Frequency*
	Spends more time with sisters	*Duration*
	Improved quality of interaction	*Rating questionnaire for sisters*
Play skills	More time engaged in independent play	*Duration*
	Uses a wider variety of toys	*Number*
Fold towels	Folds neatly	*Accuracy*
	Folds many towels	*Number*
	Folds towels more quickly	*Rate*
Greetings	Appropriately waves when Dad arrives	*Prompt level*
	More variety to greetings	*Number of types*
Making cookies with Mom	Cracks eggs	*Accuracy*
	Completely presses cookie cutter through dough	*Intensity*
Temper tantrums	Reduce number of incidents	*Frequency*
	Shorter time for each tantrum	*Duration*
Aggression to sibling	Hits less often	*Frequency*
	Does not hit so hard	*Intensity*
Your own target?	?	?

Measuring Things Done by Others

Up until now, we've focused on measuring actions taken by your child. However, you may find it valuable to measure changes involving other people, including yourself. For example, you may want your son with autism to agree to play a game suggested by your daughter. How well this skill develops depends in part upon how often your daughter initiates playing the game, and possibly how rewarding your daughter is to your son after playing the game. Similarly, how often your son asks for help will depend upon how many "needy" situations you create. If you simply wait for these situations to occur naturally, your son may not have sufficient opportunities to practice the new skill. Therefore, in addition to measuring how your son responds to your daughter's invitations to play and how often he asks for help, you should also measure how often your daughter asks your son to play and how many situations you create where your son could ask for help.

Here are some other examples where it would be useful to measure other people's actions:

- You decide to use a token system to encourage your child to use more complete sentence structure. How quickly your child acquires this new skill will depend upon how often you use the token system. Therefore, you may want to count how many tokens you've handed out in the morning.
- You want everyone in the family to ignore the latest swear word that your child has just picked up from school. In this situation, you may want to count how often each member of your family follows through by ignoring the new word. You could make a game out of this, rewarding the family member who ignores the best across the week!

Many lessons involve changing the intensity or even the type of prompt that you will use. In this case, it is the level of support that you use that you will be measuring, not whether your child actually engages in the behavior. For example, Harry is working on teaching his son, Theo, to cross the street when the light turns green. Should Harry count how often Theo successfully crosses the street? Of course not, since Harry will make certain that Theo always crosses the street in a safe manner. Instead, Harry can measure what kind of prompt he uses to assure a safe crossing, or how long before they reach the street he needs to use a particular prompt (e.g., "What will you do if the light is red? What will you do if the light is green?"). In each of these examples, we need to measure what teachers and other people are doing who interact with our children.

How Much Information Should Be Collected?

In school, you may observe teachers or specialists taking data on every opportunity or trial that they set up. Early in a lesson, when minor alterations can result in important problems in skill acquisition, collecting a lot of information can be very important. But consider this situation: you've developed a task analysis for tooth brushing that involves sixteen steps. Your child has been working on this task for almost two years and has nearly mastered this skill. In fact, she only occasionally makes a mistake on two of the steps. Should you stand there and record her performance on all sixteen steps each time she brushes her teeth? We don't think this represents a good investment of your time and effort. Recording your child's performance on the two steps in question is the only "new" information you need.

Collecting, and then studying, information about performance always involves a degree of effort and expenditure of time. As your child acquires a skill, you will most likely need far less information to assure that progress continues. Take measurements only in so far as they help you answer your primary question—is this a good lesson or should I make a change? In fact, it is possible to gather too much information. That is, you can collect information that does not help you improve the lesson. In these cases, you end up wasting your limited resources.

There are two **situations where it is important to record every occurrence of a behavior:**

1. If the behavior is especially dangerous (e.g., you are working on decreasing how often your child lights matches in the house), or
2. If the behavior is a critical new skill (e.g., you are in the first two weeks of teaching your child to ask for a break).

On the other hand, if your child currently runs around the house 150 times each day, it may be impractical to try to record them all; furthermore, it is unlikely that recording each instance will add helpful information to you. We advise you and your family to look over all of the lessons that you are planning to teach and consider these questions:

1. Which lessons are relatively new and which ones are nearly mastered?
2. Do any involve critical new skills?
3. Do any lessons target behaviors that are dangerous to your child or others?
4. Who is in the best position to record the information you deem important?

Only after you have considered these questions are you in a position to discuss how often information should be collected.

Sampling Behavior

When you decide that you do not want or need to record each occurrence of an action, you may want to use a *sampling* strategy instead. This strategy is the same used by quality assurance managers in many situations. For example, a company cannot practically test every pen nib on every pen they produce. Instead, they sample in a systematic fashion some of the pens and measure the quality of that sample. So too can you choose to sample some of your child's specific behaviors.

One sampling strategy takes advantage of units of time—called an *interval sampling* strategy. For example, rather than count each time Sonja runs around the house, Lily simply chooses to note whether any running occurred within each block of 30 minutes. If Sonja gets home from school at 4:00 PM and goes to bed at 9:00 PM, then there are 10 intervals for Lily to record. The length of the interval will depend on how often the action typically occurs. Pick a length of time during which some intervals include the target action but others do not. By comparing the number of no-running intervals to the number of intervals with running, you will be able to measure progress—more intervals without Sonja running around means things are improving in this case.

Another way to sample high rate actions is to use *spot checks*—select specific times when you will observe whether the action is occurring or not. Set a timer and when it rings, immediately observe whether the behavior being measured is taking place. For example, Raymond is teaching his son Charlie to play quietly in the family room while he is not in the room. He lets Charlie know that if he does a "good job" of playing like a big boy then he will get to watch his favorite cartoon video. Raymond leaves Charlie in the family room and sets a timer for five minutes. When it rings, he peeks into the room and notes that Charlie is still playing. He continues to spot check every five or so minutes for about 30 minutes. If Charlie has stayed in the room for 80 percent of the spot checks, he gets to watch the video. In this manner, Raymond does not have to observe everything his son is doing but can still accurately track Charlie's progress.

Product or Outcome Reviews

Another way to monitor performance without directly observing your child is to measure the outcome or product of a task. For example, when Lucy tells Shelby to clean her bedroom, she does not have to watch what Shelby is doing. Instead, at a set time later, she can come into the room and determine how clean the room is. If the bed is neatly made, the clothes are put away in the proper place, the toys are stored correctly, and the floor is swept, then Lucy can decide that Shelby did a good job of cleaning. Similarly, if Lucy tells Shelby to get dressed, she does not have to watch Shelby getting dressed. Instead, she can set standards that are associated with proper dressing—zippers and buttons are closed, shirt is tucked neatly into pants, etc. Likewise, once Shelby has learned the basic steps of setting the table, Lucy will not need to watch her doing this. Instead, she can check whether all the plates and dinnerware have been properly set. You can readily see that using this type of strategy will help reduce time you spend measuring performance.

Charting and Summarizing

Taking measurements regarding your child's actions is only beneficial if it reveals information that helps you decide what to do about your lesson strategy. If the information indicates that steady progress has been made, then you will not want to change your strategy. If your information shows that little or no progress has been made, then you will need to consider revamping your lesson strategy. Therefore, the information collected needs to be summarized in a manner that helps you see the basic direction or *trend* of your child's performance. Converting raw numbers into a visual model—a chart, graph, or table—is one way to help you find trends.

A chart or graph can be made by creating a grid noting your measurement information on one axis (the Y-axis, or the vertical axis) and noting time on the other axis (the X-axis, or horizontal axis). A line graph is made by using a single point to represent each piece of information (data), while a bar graph is made by filling in the space below a specific level. If you do not want to create the graph by hand, there are many user-friendly software programs (including Microsoft Excel®) that can help you create graphs and determine a trend line. If you do not use a program to find the trend line, then you may want to use some relatively simple strategies to note trends.

For example, Sidney is focusing on helping Sara increase the number of spontaneous requests she makes at home. He notes her progress by charting the number of spontaneous requests per day for ten days. Then he estimates the mid-point of the first three points and places an X at that point and does the same for the last three points. He then connects these lines to create a trend-line. He extends that line

Graph 8-1 | Using Estimated Mid-points to Plot a Trend Line

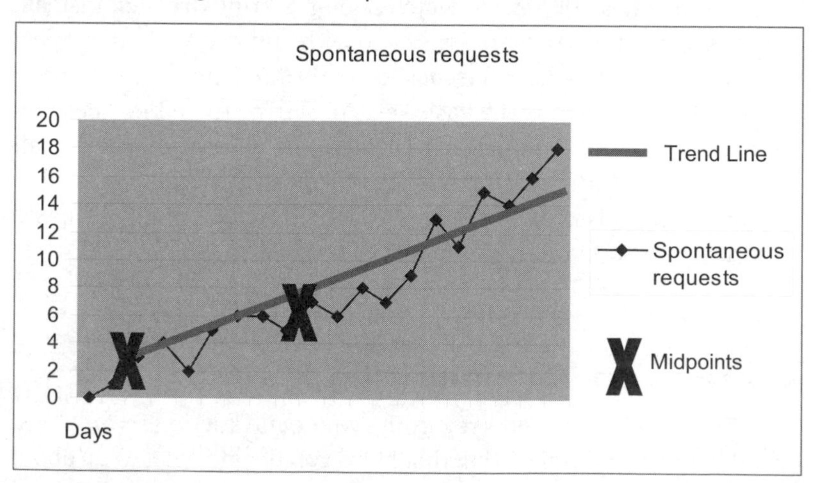

Graph 8-2 | Number of Pictures Mastered within PECS

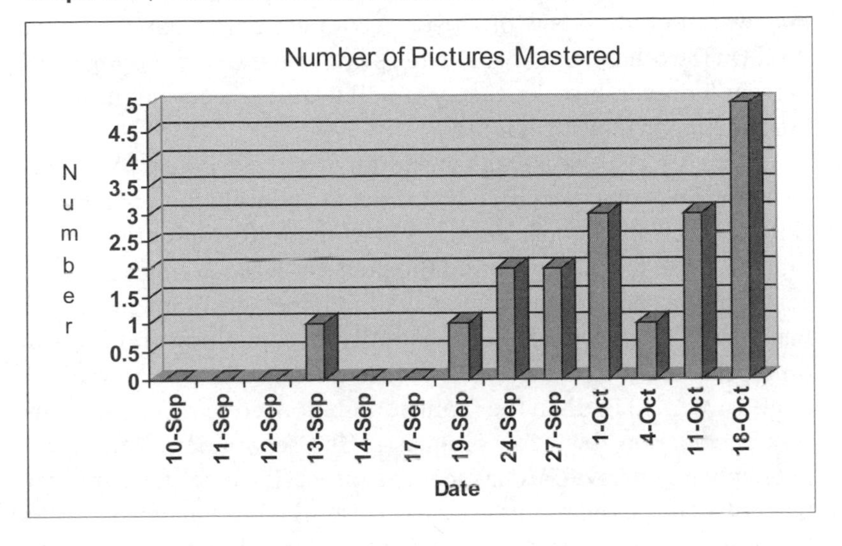

on the chart and then looks to make sure that subsequent points are at or *above* that line. He knows that if the points start to consistently fall below that line, then Sara's progress would not be maintained. In the example shown in Graph 8-1, you can see that the points after the second X largely remain above that line. If you are trying to reduce a CIB, then you would be checking to see whether your points are remaining *below* your trend line. While there are more stringent and statistically powerful ways to find a trend line, this strategy typically is useful enough for family purposes.

Another strategy to chart progress is shown in Graph 8-2, which uses a bar graph approach. In this case, Sam is monitoring the number of pictures that John-Paul uses within his PECS communication book. Although there are some ups and downs from day to day, the overall pattern is clearly one that shows nice progress.

When you design a task analysis, you can place an area to graph your results on the same page where you list the sequence of steps in your task. Your graph can indicate the number of steps that your child performed without any help or prompting. For example, if your task analysis has 14 steps and your child performs 7 of these independently, then you would note 50 percent for that day. Since different tasks are associated with a different number of steps, using percent independent will allow you to compare progress across vastly different types of goals. If you see that your child performs at 90 percent on a task, you may want to reduce how often you record her performance on that task. On the other hand, if your child's performance is hovering at 25 percent for several weeks, then you will want to reconsider how you are teaching that particular task.

You can also use a graph or similar visual aid to help you determine the level of expectation you want to maintain for a particular skill or CIB. For example, James is aiming for his son Carl to spontaneously ask for things around the house at least 10 times per day. James puts a chart on the kitchen wall that includes 10 open circles. Each time Carl asks anyone in the family for something without any prompting from them, they fill in one of the circles. When all 10 circles are filled in, then the family does not need to record any further information about Carl's requests. On a separate log, James can note how many days Carl has met the target. If the target is met for 8 out of 10 days, then James slightly raises the level of expectations for requests and tracks this increased level by adding more circles to the chart on the kitchen wall.

This strategy can be used to note your child's progress on behavioral goals when the goal is to achieve a level *below* a certain number. For example, Char knows that Jack frequently turns on the kitchen faucet to play with the water; he does this at least 20 times each day. While Char would like him to stop completely, she realizes it will take some time to achieve such a dramatic change. She also knows that if Jack turned the water on only 15 times, that would be a better day. She places 16 tokens on the refrigerator and tells Jack that if there is at least one token remaining by 8:30 PM (30 minutes before he starts his bedtime routines), then he will be able to have a favorite ice cream treat. Each time Jack turns on the faucet, Char removes one of the tokens and reminds him how he can earn the ice cream. If all the tokens have been removed by 8:30, Char does not allow him this treat. She records how many days he is successful at earning his treat. When he reaches four days in a row, she lowers the target level by one token. This way, she does not have to record each time she removes a token. She only needs to note how often the overall strategy is successful on a day-to-day basis. And her chart about successful days lets her quickly see when she should change the requirement for Jack's treat. This strategy is obviously similar to the token/point systems we described in Chapter 2.

Review

The evaluation strategies discussed in this chapter are truly the core of the Pyramid Approach. If we don't evaluate what we are doing, we can waste our own time and that of our children. Teaching your child new skills and reducing or eliminating problematic behaviors involves a great deal of time and effort on your part. To help assure that you are best using your resources, you must evaluate what you are doing. When we design a lesson or an intervention for a contextually inappropriate behavior, we can only guess what will be effective—we cannot guarantee the outcome. Therefore, plan to collect information in a manner that will help you decide whether you should continue with your current plan or modify it.

Once you've collected your information, you will need a system to help you analyze that information so that you will make sound decisions about your strategies.

The steps we should take to help evaluate skill development lesson plans are:

1. Pick a way to measure the target skill.
2. Try out your measurement system (does it make sense and appear reliable?).
3. Choose a level of success—X level by Y date—remembering that success can be measured by changes in rate, intensity, accuracy, duration, number, amount of prompting needed (e.g., "This is working!").
4. Choose a level of failure—Z level by Y date (e.g., "This is not working.").
5. Implement your teaching strategy.
6. Use your measurement system.
7. Evaluate your outcome and compare it to your expectation.
8. If you are successful, keep going.
9. If you are not successful, what will you change? Review your goal for your child, the reinforcers you are using, the types of prompts, and the other elements of lessons discussed in earlier chapters.

The final chapter of this book offers suggestions on how you can integrate the full Pyramid Approach into all the activities associated with living at home and in the community.

Pulling It Together in the Neighborhood

Teresa has worked hard to make her home a place where Zena and Crystal, her two teenage children with autism, can learn and still have a lot of fun. She dreads going out into the community, however, because her children find many places too novel and unpredictable. Crystal, who uses speech to communicate, seems readily frightened; Zena, who uses PECS to communicate in short sentences, seems oblivious to danger. Teresa wonders how she will be able to take her children safely into the community while also teaching them the many skills they will need to make a good adjustment into the adult world.

We've discussed several strategies to promote many skills in a variety of situations in and around the home. We will now focus on how you can use these same strategies away from home, when you are visiting your favorite locales in the neighborhood. We will consider recreational activities, shopping and other service-oriented settings, family visits (including during special occasions such as holidays), and some options while on vacation (both at home and while away). We also will review mealtime issues, both at home and out in the community.

Recreational Settings

For your child to fit into recreational settings in the community, he needs to know:

1. how to use community equipment and facilities appropriately;
2. how to play with other children in a way that they perceive as appropriate and friendly.

It may be difficult to combine the two skills immediately, because if a child does not know how to play with something such as a swing or slide, other children may not be interested in playing with him.

Let's look at how you might begin to teach these skills at a community playground. As with teaching other skills, we strongly suggest that when you arrange to teach your child to use the play equipment, you have no other obligations at the time (such as monitoring your other children or wanting to work on interactive play skills). You may even want to arrange to visit the playground when it is deserted to help you and your child focus on the equipment. We also encourage you to use something to motivate your child and permit him to request breaks or help during play time. Remember, although we hope that children will learn to have fun, some may be less than thrilled with their initial lessons at the playground.

To use most types of playground equipment, children need to do many steps in a particular order—such as climb up the ladder, sit down on the top of the slide, let go of the bars, slide down, and land on their feet. As with many other sequential lessons, you may want to start by helping your child fully with the first steps and expecting him to learn to be independent with the last steps. In the case of the slide, you would first remind your child about the potential reward— either how much fun sliding is or perhaps something he will receive when he gets to the bottom. Then, help your child climb up the ladder and get into position on the slide, and finally encourage him to let go. Hopefully, you (or somebody else) will be at the bottom to enthusiastically meet your sliding child! Over time, you will gradually reduce your help in climbing and letting go.

Turn Taking

Once your child has learned all the steps involved in sliding and can do them independently, it is time to teach about turn taking. Your child may have already learned about turn taking while playing at home. For some children, however, the community may be the first place they need to use this skill. Ask another child (a sibling or relative, perhaps) to play, but be sure to make it clear that your child is just learning to take turns and may appear to be "rude" at first. Be sure to praise both children for taking turns. You may want to encourage each child to communicate to the other child, "Your turn" (regardless of the mode of communication).

For this lesson to be most effective, choose equipment that involves activities that have a clear start and stop point. Using a slide involves climbing the stairs and then sliding down and thus has natural break points. In contrast, if a child can swing by himself, then he can sustain that activity for a long time. You would have to interfere with his swinging to get him off the swings, and that may not be easy to accomplish at first. For the slide, while your child is sliding down, the other child could move to the bottom of the stairs. When your child gets to the stair bottom to climb up again, you can encourage him to communicate that it is the other child's turn, and learn to take his turn after the other child completes his slide down.

During this time, if you have been using any arbitrary rewards for sliding, be sure to try to minimize their use in order to promote the social consequences associated with playing with friends. If your child has learned to use and enjoy other equipment, you may want to build in opportunities for the children to alternate selecting which piece of equipment will next be used.

In general, add only one new piece of equipment on each day of training. Once your child has learned to play on one or two pieces, you can start the playtime with using whatever he likes best before trying to introduce a new play routine. That is, let him use his favorite routine first, then teach him to use some other equipment before letting him return to the one he most likes. In fact, access to a favorite piece of equipment will probably serve as a good reward for learning how to use a new piece of equipment.

Remember that if your child especially likes the playground, at some point you will want to leave! So, do not surprise your child with an announcement that it is time to go home. Set that up at the very start of playtime. You can set a timer or use activity-cards/pictures to indicate when you will leave. For children who like several activities, you may want to use "tickets"—3 tickets for the slides means three rides, 2 tickets on the jungle gym means 2 times climbing all the way around, etc. If your child understands time, then be sure to set the time before you start to play—otherwise, leaving will seem like a "surprise" to your child and he may not like that. You may want to use a type of transitional object or other visual cue associated with a reward for doing (or starting) the next activity. For example, perhaps your child picked out a favorite audiotape or CD before you left your car to go onto the playground. When it is time to go home, you can take out the tape and give it to your child while he is still on the playground. He's likely to take you back to the car so that he can listen to his favorite tape!

If you go to a new playground, you may want to determine first which equipment your child knows and likes to use. You also want to assure yourself that the equipment is as safe as what you use in your neighborhood. Some slides are made of plastic derivatives and do not get very hot even in the direct sun, while other slides are made of metal and can become scorching hot. You should also check if there is room around the equipment. Can your child safely walk past other kids who are swinging? Remember, your child is not likely to be as aware of safety issues as you are, so be his eyes when first appraising a new location.

The playground is a natural place to work on communication skills. For example, your child may have difficulty using a piece of equipment or may need a boost to get started. These are great times to work on having him ask for "help." Of course, if your child is playing with other children, you will want to encourage him to ask for help from his friends. Don't forget to work on receptive communication skills such as following simple instructions from both adults and children—for example, "Let's play in the sandbox" or "Hey, give me the shovel!"

While you want your child to enjoy playing with other children, this goal may represent a challenge from his perspective. In this case, asking for a quiet break would be appropriate. You may want to bring a timer to help set limits on alone-play time.

You may want to plan how and where you will deal with inappropriate behavior on the playground. If you use time out at home, then you will want to plan to use a specific location for your TO area in the park—possibly a bench or a spot near a fence where your child can sit quietly for a moment. It is important to plan for problems rather than be surprised if you see actions out in the community that you sometimes see at home. This is also why it is most important to be sure that you have arranged for some powerful reinforcers to be available for your child's appropriate behaviors as well as support for any communication system that your child uses. For example, if your child uses PECS, then you must be sure that his communication book and the necessary vocabulary pictures are available at all times while out in the community.

Attending Quiet Events

Teaching children to go to the movies or attend events at places of worship can be tricky because other people usually have high standards regarding proper decorum. First, it is important to separate times when you feel that you *must* go versus times you are attending to teach something to your child. In the second situation, you should be willing to leave if your child cannot handle the entire event, but in the first case, you will feel very stressed if you leave (or possibly very embarrassed if you stay!).

Here is one strategy that we have found effective when we take children with autism spectrum disorders into the community in order to teach a skill. Rather than start the activity the same time everyone else does, do something else with your child at the start (including practicing things that might come up at the end of the activity) and then join the group near the end. This way, your child will only have to successfully participate in some of the event but can enjoy finishing with everyone else. Over time, try to bring your child into the event earlier and earlier.

Before beginning the activity, remember to have your child select something that he would like upon finishing the activity—hopefully, something that can be shared with others, but, if necessary, something that is unique for your child. You may need a visual system to remind your child how long the activity will last. If he can't use a watch or clock to tell time, try a type of token-system using the tokens as markers for the passage of time.

For example, if your child has never been to a movie theater and you are not sure he can sit and watch a 90-minute movie, then be sure to bring some highly motivating items, since you cannot be certain that the movie alone will be motivating. Furthermore, rather than bringing your child into the start of the movie and seeing how long he can last, you may want to bring him in just 15 minutes before the end and then reward him richly for "staying until the end." If he likes popcorn, then you can slowly distribute the popcorn throughout the time that he is watching the movie. The next time you go to the movies, you can try to have him see the last 30 minutes, then 45, etc. Of course, this is not a natural way to watch a movie, but the point is not to see this particular movie but to teach your child how to successfully "go to the movies." When he learns this skill, there will be plenty of movies that you can watch together from beginning to end!

Since you are going to the movie specifically to learn that skill, if your child acts inappropriately, you can choose to take him out and end that opportunity. Of course, if your child was trying to get out of the theater, then it would be better to teach him to ask for a break. This would allow him to get out for a moment or so, but then return and try to earn the reward you've set up.

There are other places in the community that often require children to be quiet for some or all of the time. Many religious services have noisy periods (e.g., singing) as well as quiet times (e.g., silent devotions). Before attending a quiet event, be sure to consider what type of reinforcing activity your child can engage in while everyone else is being quiet. Food may not be permitted, so you may need to choose other types of rewards, such as coloring or sticker books, or even tokens. It will be helpful to involve the community elders/leaders so they can see that you are trying to establish routines that should ultimately benefit the entire community.

Service-Oriented Settings

Parents frequently must take their children to locations in the community that provide special services—places such as the barber, clothing or shoe store, the library, and various medical providers. Families visit some of these places on a routine basis—such as for a monthly haircut—but others only on an as-needed basis—such as to see the doctor. For these service-oriented settings, it is helpful to plan time to teach your child the routines of the location on a day when you do not really need the services.

Stores

In previous chapters, we discussed strategies for teaching your child about going to the grocery store. Food shopping is something most families do fairly often, so children need to learn how to tolerate grocery stores pretty early on. But your child will also eventually need to learn how to behave and what to do at stores that your family patronizes less often—such as clothing or shoe stores.

You may want to take your child to a clothing or shoe store when you do not need to buy something. Just as when you are teaching your child about the playground, you will probably want to arrange to come to the store at a time when not many other people are around. Before entering the store, have your child pick out a reward that he would like. Then choose a very easy goal—perhaps to sit in a chair and simply hold a pair of shoes without even trying them on. Reward your child for a job well done and quickly leave. On the next visit, extend what you expect of your child—perhaps to have one foot measured, for example. Be sure that what you provide as a reward is more important to him than the shoe—if he thinks he gets every shoe he tries on, shopping will be difficult!

Over time, you may want your child to help you determine whether things fit. To begin this type of lesson, you might start with exaggerated errors. For example, have your child try on a shoe that is far too small or one that is far too big; a shirt that is too small to even so large that the arms are almost hanging to the floor. Praise your child for rejecting the things that do not fit and for selecting ones that do fit. Of course, if your child has distinct preferences for colors or styles, incorporate choosing things in his favorite color or style into the activity. You may be able to practice some of the activities at home before trying them in the store. For example, perhaps the shoe store manager would lend you a measuring tool. Still, you must remember to use your rewards when you change from practicing activities at home to actually doing them at the store, even if you think your child is comfortable with the routine.

Healthcare Settings

If you are going to the dentist's office—something that you will do many times over the years!—arrange with your dentist for a practice run. One friendly dentist that we know allows the child to simply sit in the chair for the first visit before receiving some type of reward. On the next visit, he tries to get the child to open his mouth and allow him to simply tap—not poke or prod—on each tooth with a pick. He might introduce the child to his equipment. Our friendly dentist uses "Mr. Thirsty" and "Mr. Tickler" as names for the suction device and the tooth polisher. Over the next several visits, he gradually does more "real" work, but allows the child to stop him by asking for a break. Yes, this process takes some time but most dentists view their contact with a family as something to be cultivated over time and will gladly cooperate if you talk about this strategy. Because you may need several "trial runs," talk to the office about why this is important in the long run so that they won't charge you for each visit!

If your child is comforted at home by "deep pressure"—he likes to wrap himself tightly in a blanket, etc.—have the dentist put the lead apron used during x-rays over your child during the visit.

You may also want to put time into practice trips to the doctor's office— going there, sitting in the waiting area, and leaving without even seeing the doctor. If the visit involves use of something novel, such as a tongue depressor or pressure cuff, try to arrange for an opportunity to use it at home with your child before the doctor or nurse must use it with him. If your child can use a schedule at home, you can bring a mini-schedule to the doctor's office, noting sequences such as:

1. Wait in the outer room
2. Sit in the examination room
3. Greet doctor/nurse
4. Step on scale
5. Have nurse take blood pressure/measure heart rate
6. Doctor looks in ears
7. Doctor looks in mouth and down throat
8. Add as necessary

Note: visits to the barber (or hair stylist!) can likewise begin with short visits aimed at helping your child become acquainted with the setting, the chairs, the combs, brushes, scissors, dryers, and other common equipment before having his hair cut.

Another tricky aspect of many healthcare locales is dealing with the dreaded waiting room. You have a 2 o'clock appointment but you know you will not be seeing the doctor at that precise time. In fact, your doctor is fairly certain of the same fact and has arranged for a separate waiting area—and has placed relatively boring magazines for you to read there if, by chance, you did not bring yourself something to do.

So, since you can anticipate that you must wait, you must anticipate the same for your child. It is not likely that the magazines will be enticing to your child. Many pediatricians have toys in the waiting room, but these, too, may not be appealing to your child. Therefore, you must bring along something that your child enjoys doing and can engage in while not be highly disruptive to the other people waiting. In Chapter 3, we talked about the importance of the "wait" lesson, and here is where its fruits will be the sweetest! But remember, this is not the location to start the wait lesson since you do not control how long the wait will last and such control is the key to creating a successful lesson. Be sure to have your child select a potential reward before you enter the doctor's or dentist's office area, and make sure it is something you can provide quickly once you leave.

Libraries

Libraries can be interesting community settings for children with autism. Some children like these settings because the expectation is for relatively little communication via talking—being quiet is a virtue here! Of course, for other children, this requirement is a problem, as they enjoy being noisy. If this is the case for your child, then you may want to practice visiting the library when there are few other patrons on hand—perhaps just upon opening.

You may want to work on the initial goals for learning how to use a library just as we described for going shopping. That is, on your first trip, quickly locate and check out one book that you know your child will enjoy and read it as soon as possible. On subsequent trips, gradually spend more time looking for books (including ones that you want) before getting the book that he wants. You can also choose to spend some time using other library resources such as copy machines or computers.

One clever mom hid a McDonald's coupon in a library book and taught her child to quietly search through the pages to find the coupon. Over time, she would give her child more books to look through and occasionally hid other items that were fun for the child but not associated with going out for a snack.

Visiting Family and Friends

Taking your children to visit relatives and other acquaintances can be richly rewarding—or highly stressful! Fundamentally, children will do best when they feel secure and believe that they can trust their surroundings, including other people. Over time, almost all children can learn that the rules at Grandma's home are different than those at home, but that they are consistent and can be followed. How to reach that point of comfort may involve many steps.

As we've tried to note, children do well at home (and in the community and at school) when they: 1) are engaged in functional activities, 2) have a clear system of reinforcement in place, and 3) have support for their communication skills, both expressive and receptive. If your child has learned to follow a visual schedule at school and at home, then take the schedule with you when you visit other people, indicating what activities will take place, including when you will go back home. (See, for example, Figure 3-2 on page 53.)

If you use a token system for rewards (or a puzzle or point system), be sure to take that with you as well. And if your child uses a visually based communication system (such as PECS or an electronic device) be sure that system is available whenever you leave the house. If your child uses sign language, be sure that you've taught your relatives how to respond to the most important signs. If your child's reinforcement and communication system are available in the new setting, this support will minimize the novel—and thus potentially frightening—aspects of going away from home.

Remember that despite your efforts to calm your child, he might become upset in the new situation. Therefore, plan how (and where) you will give your child an opportunity to take a break (or simply get away) from either specific activities or specific people. That is, if the routines for dinner are new (and possibly slower) than at home, you should allow your child the chance to request a break and be permitted to leave the dining room for a short time. If your child feels there is no escape, then you will see a dramatic escalation of problematic behaviors. For example, if you go to a relative's home for Thanksgiving dinner, plan for an area where your child can take a quiet break, especially if he is likely to react to the hustle and bustle associated with so many new people around him. You should take care that the food served will not be too novel or that you've brought along some favorites that might help coax your child to sample some new fare.

When we think of visiting our grandmother's, we usually smile in anticipation of all the nice things she will give us, even when we really don't deserve them! You may want to help your child learn how rewarding it can be to visit other people. That is, have the people you visit immediately provide some reinforcers for your child even before putting any demands upon him. If you're not sure they will have things that your child likes, bring rewarding items with you but let them hand the rewards out. In time, you (and those you are visiting) can gradually increase your expectations for your child's participation in various activities and routines, or for simply being polite.

Be sure to bring "filler" activities—things your child has learned to do relatively independently, and, hopefully, with enjoyment. Then, when everyone else is helping to set the table with the heirloom china that no five-year-old should handle, you will have something else your child can do. If you merely hope your child will "stay out of trouble," that expectation is doomed to fail, given enough time!

When visiting someone's home for the first time, be sure to check whether there are any pets that may frighten your child or cause allergic reactions, or that your child may aggravate! If other children will be present, you may want to arrange for some time to talk about your child and any of his unique characteristics. Openness and candor should be the rule, along with high expectations all around.

Routine Visits

If you are visiting relatives or friends and you anticipate that such visits will become routine, then it is important to develop some routines for that location. You may want to consider activities that your child can engage in that require minimum supervision so that you will have time to spend with whomever you are visiting. If these activities require materials not likely to be where you are going, then be sure to take them along.

Let your child know if there are any areas that are "off limits" to him—either for safety or privacy reasons. If you use portable locks to secure certain areas of your home, you may want to bring some and ask your friends or relatives if you can use them in such special places.

Asking for Breaks. You may also want to designate a special "quiet" area—somewhere that your child can calmly escape to if circumstances become overwhelming (e.g., many unfamiliar guests continue to show up and they're all trying to talk to your child).

One creative mother we knew taught her son Josh to ask for a break at home. He became quite independent at quietly asking for a break when events in the home became stressful for him. His mother created a special "break chair" for him in a quiet part of the house. When his mother took him out in the community, though, Josh didn't seem to generalize this skill to novel environments. Josh's mom thought that this could be because she couldn't take Josh's break chair with her. So, she began putting a bright yellow cloth napkin on the break chair at home, and Josh continued taking breaks at home. Then, when she went into the community, she took the yellow napkin with her, and she made sure that Josh saw her take it from his chair when they left the house. Josh quickly learned to ask for a break in the community, and when he did so, his mother put the yellow napkin down in whatever quiet area she could quickly find, and Josh happily sat on it while he "cooled down."

Video Modeling. To teach your child social skills that would be useful at a specific friend's or relative's house, consider using video modeling, as described in Chapter 5. For example, when Phil went to visit his grandparents, he immediately ran to the video game room. Although his grandparents had set this area up for Phil, they were always disappointed that he did not greet them when he came into their home. His parents decided to videotape a scene in which his brother (playing the role of Phil) greeted their next-door neighbor (playing the role of his grandparents) as he entered the neighbor's house. Next, they taught Phil a three-turn social greeting script, as modeled by his brother in the video, and had him practice this at home. They also sent the script to his grandparents. On Phil's next visit there, his grandparents met him at the door while holding his favorite video game and then proceeded through the script. Phil took his turn appropriately in the script, greeting his grandparents and answering their question about how he was doing. After this "proper" greeting, Phil ran down to play his game.

Scripts. There are a variety of social scripts that may be helpful to your child—in a variety of situations, not just when visiting friends and relatives. A script is like learning the lines within a play. And just as actors first rehearse their lines before trying them out before the audience, so too would children learn their lines within a role-playing situation before using them in real life situations. How the script is presented will have a great deal to do with your child's skills. Some children can be taught their "part" simply by observing a model and then imitating and repeating what the model did. Other children are able to read, so following a written script can be helpful for them. It also is important to teach children several scripts or different ways to effectively handle a situation so that the outcome does not appear to be too artificial. For example, if you want your child to learn how to respond to questions about seeing a movie, be sure that your child eventually learns to talk about different movies with different people.

Visitors in Your Home. Many parents wonder how they can tell visitors to their home about their child's special needs or traits. Borrowing from a strategy observed at her son's school, Denyse posted a few key reminders under the "Welcome to my Home" sign by her front door. The first asked visitors to look directly at her son when talking to him. The second note asked them *not* to look at her son if he was throwing a tantrum. You may want to similarly post any special instructions you'd like visitors to your home to follow.

Mealtimes

Most of us look forward to a quiet, relaxing meal with the other members of our family. It is a time to share good food and to talk about things that are important within the family or simply just fun to discuss. Unfortunately, mealtimes also can be stressful times for everyone. Some people may feel rushed and ready to move to the next activity, while others may be upset about things that happened that day (or will soon happen) and thus not want to talk to anyone. And some children with autism may not enjoy family discussions or may be distracted by the foods, smells, or routines associated with the meal. What can parents do to minimize stress and promote a relaxed atmosphere?

Learning about Mealtime Routines

Let's first consider routine meals and then we'll consider common exceptions. At breakfast time, everyone is often running around getting ready for the day and spending little time as a group. Sitting alone and eating a bowl of cereal is a fairly common routine in many families. If this scenario is true for your family, then you may not need to require a great deal of social interaction during the meal. You will want to determine how much of the routine you'd like your child to directly participate in, remembering that the more he gets involved in the routine, the fewer opportunities he will have to engage in inappropriate actions. Depending upon your child's age and skill level, you should expect some participation in some of the routines—for example, taking a plastic bowl from the counter to the table and getting a spoon from the drawer and a napkin from the holder. You may want to speed up certain aspects to help avoid problems—for example, you may want to pour milk from the gallon container into a cup for your child to pour into his cereal bowl or put some cereal into a large bowl for transfer to his bowl (instead of expecting him to handle the large cereal box).

You should consider what else your child can do while eating his breakfast. Will you have time to review his day with him, either by simply talking about what will occur or by reviewing a visual schedule? If you don't have much interaction time, can he look at a book (picture or otherwise) or something else without this interfering dramatically with finishing eating? Remember, it is likely that you do other things while eating your breakfast, such as reading the newspaper or watching the sports review on TV. Thus, it will be important to gradually teach your child about appropriate activities he can do while having breakfast.

Be sure to have your child participate in some manner in cleaning up, even if only to put his spoon in the basket in the dishwasher. If your child has trouble finishing his breakfast within a reasonable time, you can use a timer, clock, or some other visual aid to help him note the progress of time. Of course, when he does finish on time, he should receive some prearranged reward—even if just your joyful praise!

Dinners may be more complex because there may be more social demands associated with having more family members present at this meal. As with all meals, plan which parts of the dinner routine you'd like your child to participate in—from setting up to cleaning up. To prevent your child from developing rituals, you may want to make a visual (or written) chart with many jobs related to dinnertime and rotate through the possible activities throughout the week.

Communicating during Meals

You should expect communication to be part of dinner, with your child expressing himself (using whichever modality) and also listening to others. Everyone needs to learn to ask for and share various common items, from specific foods to utensils and other materials. Remember to encourage your child to initiate communication, not just to respond to or imitate others. Dinnertime is also a great time to encourage communication between siblings, so try to avoid having the parents (or other adults) control all of the interactions. If there are topics you routinely discuss—from what happened at school that day to what the family will be doing on the weekend—then it may help to rehearse these issues/topics before the meal with your child.

Having a visual script (either written or pictorial) may help your child when it is his turn to communicate. For example, the script can contain information about topics that your child can talk about or areas of interest of other people in the group. Perhaps a word or picture will help your child remember that Uncle Bob likes to talk about baseball or that Aunt Sue just took a trip to Australia. The script can also help your child recall interesting things or events that he has recently participated in.

If your child can communicate quite well but isn't sure what to talk about, or if he talks about issues that are inappropriate or just too ritualistic, then you may want to prepare a simple list of topics to discuss during dinner. With such a list, you can also encourage your child to cross out or erase topics that have been covered in order to promote variation both within and across meals. You can also introduce topics that you want to include—upcoming visits to relatives, important events at school such as parties or tests, changes in routines involving visitors to your home, etc. If these types of changes stress your child, you may want to introduce them before the meal so that when they are brought up at dinner time, they are not novel items for him to adjust to while everyone is present.

If your child is stressed by aspects of the dinner—either the social or activity routines—then set up a system to reward him for participating in portions of the meal in such a way that he can tell when the meal will be finished. Be sure to permit him to use some of the critical skills noted in Chapter 3, such as asking for a break or help.

Dinner Guests

Whenever possible, plan for changes in your normal family mealtime routines, whether you have a single guest coming over for one meal or are confronting wholesale changes, such as during holiday dinners. Not only should you work with your child to cope with your dinner guest, but you may want to offer advice to your guest prior to the start of the meal. Bearing in mind what your child likes to talk about, you can offer suggestions on topics that will promote interaction between the guest and your child. You may want to offer advice on whether the style of your guest will fit the style of your child. For example, you can warn Uncle Dave, who likes to slap people on the back as a sign of friendship, that your child tends to react to such contact as aggressive or frightening. You also can find out from your guest some topics she enjoys talking about—what she likes to eat, where she has traveled recently—and prepare your child to talk about these issues.

Eating Out

Going out for a meal can be very stressful for children with autism. From your child's perspective, there may be nothing fast about "fast-food" restaurants, especially at peak times. These locales involve many strangers, from those working at the site to other customers, many of whom will expect some communicative interaction with your child. If your child is very young or appears quite stressed at such places, you should consider going to them only when there are the shortest lines possible. You also should plan what your child will order before getting in line and consider something quick and easy. For example, rather than buying a full meal, just buy some French fries and eat them quickly. Review the routines of different restaurants with your child so he knows what to expect. For example, will your child be handed a drink or will he be given an empty cup to fill? Over time, order fuller meals and visit the restaurant when more people are around.

As noted before, consider the first trips as teaching time, not eating time. If a serious problem arises, end the trip and offer your child something to eat that is less appealing than the fast-food option. Consider what went wrong and then plan accordingly to modify the next outing. For example, if the line was too long, consider reviewing the "wait" lesson. If your child screamed because someone was sitting too close, either choose a spot further away from crowds on the next trip or offer your child more rewards for tolerating people being close by.

Sit-down restaurants offer different challenges than fast-food places do. For example, rather than ordering at a counter, your child will probably need to communicate with a server and select from a menu. You may want to rehearse these routines at home. Most restaurants will lend you a menu so your child can have an opportunity to review what's on it and how to use it before you enter the restaurant. Plan for what to do during the time between ordering and food being served. What relatively quiet activities can your child do at the table? What will you do if your child eats more quickly than you do? Are there rewards you can offer to your child for staying quietly with you until everyone has finished their meal?

In general, remember that mealtime is not simply food-time. There are many expectations for social interaction during meals and these issues may involve considerable stress for your child, even if he enjoys the food that is offered within the meal. When out in the community, will your child's manner of communication be readily understood by everyone else? Do you have a back-up plan if his communication attempts initially fail? Finally, what rewards will you be able to give your child during the meal and for completing the meal, both at home and out in the community? For some children, simply eating the food will not be sufficiently rewarding to motivate them to use the many skills that will be expected of them.

Going on Vacation

Going on vacation should involve fun and excitement for everyone, and possibly some calm moments as well. Unfortunately, we know of many families who virtually dread holidays and vacations. In our previous examples, we suggested doing "test runs" whenever possible—arranging for opportunities for your child to learn skills without expecting him to complete everything all at once. The problem with vacations is that there may be no opportunity to practice going to Disney World or a mountain resort. In such situations, it is still important to bring strategies into the novel situations that promote stability and routine—for example, reward systems, schedule systems, other types of communication systems if they are used, and possibly reminders about behaviors you are working on changing (and alternatives).

Whenever possible, try to obtain promotional materials related to where you will be traveling. Review the materials with your child by using visual aids (pictures, videos, etc.), written materials where appropriate, and general discussions. Before the trip, review what special vocabulary you may need—items to request (including novel foods, toys, or activities such as rides), novel things to talk about, including special places (mountains, snow, canyons, etc.), or other novel things your child will experience. Many amusement parks and other well-organized attractions promote special conditions for those with disabilities, especially if you contact them ahead of time. These may include passes to circumvent long lines, or even a special guide to help everyone enjoy the events.

Whenever you go to new locations, be sure to plan for the unexpected. That is, talk to everyone in the family about what to do in case of emergencies such as injuries, someone getting lost, or your child having a temper tantrum. In the midst of a chaotic and scary situation it will be difficult to calmly think of a plan. Be sure to secure identifying information with your child, something that someone else (including the police) would quickly find if your child is not able to fully communicate about the situation. Whether such information is on a card inside a wallet or on a bracelet or necklace would depend on what you know about your child's tendency to remove such items. To counter these tendencies, give your child frequent praise and rewards for having the ID on at all times in the community. And remember that your child may not be able to produce his best skills if the situation is stressful; thus, always have a backup plan. This information should include a way to contact you as quickly as possible (as via a cell phone, for example).

We recommend teaching children to remain still if they get lost. After all, it will not be helpful if your child is trying to find you while you are trying to find him. You also will have to make decisions about what you want your child to do if he becomes lost and someone else approaches him—should he talk or should he continue to wait for someone he recognizes? As with any skill, you should arrange to practice what to do if your child gets lost while you are in a safe environment. For example, when you have several people with you to assure safety, abruptly walk away from your child in a supermarket (with both ends of the aisle monitored) and reward your child for standing still until you return. If he tries to walk out of the aisle, try again but with a shorter interval of time for him to wait for your return. If you think your child will understand a story about dealing with being lost, you may want to read it with him to help him learn how to handle the situation.

Dealing with Holidays

Dealing with holidays can be stressful, even if your family is staying at home. Routines change, people come and go—including people your child may rarely see—strange food, costumes, customs, and other alterations become the rule rather than the exception! The key to helping your child cope with these novelties is to take advantage of calm times to teach better tolerance for change. If you put all your effort into maintaining a fixed routine virtually all the time, when change comes—and it must!—your child will not have the skills to manage it in a calm fashion.

Many of the communication skills described in Chapter 3 will hold the key regarding how well everyone will deal with holidays. For example, in the section on teaching children to follow schedules, we noted the importance of teaching the concept of "surprise." If you've spent time teaching this as part of your everyday routine, you'll find many opportunities to inform your child of surprises throughout any holiday. Likewise, being able to ask for a break will be important when your child is overwhelmed by sudden changes or the introduction of new foods, activities, or people.

Giving and receiving gifts is a part of many holidays, and you can anticipate that your child may not like everything he receives. You should not expect to teach your child how to deal with being disappointed by a gift in a room filled with your relatives. Instead, you can help prepare your child for this possibility by offering him surprise "gifts" within your normal home routines, being sure to include some duds! In this way, not only can your child be taught how to say, "Thanks!" for well-appreciated gifts but he can also practice how to politely (though less enthusiastically!) say, "Thank you!" for any gift.

Many holidays involve wearing special clothes, whether it is a Halloween costume or a shirt, jacket, and tie or a fancy dress. Have your child wear these unique items at times prior to the required time and you will have a better chance at rewarding him or her for tolerating the new attire.

We should also recognize that during holidays parents have many responsibilities—from preparing and setting out food, to talking to relatives and friends, to helping older relatives who need more attention. All of these factors will tend to decrease the amount of time and attention you will be able to devote to your child. How will he react to this change? To help your child cope when you cannot devote a lot of time to him, plan to provide him with access to a variety of reinforcing activities and materials that he can use independently.

You also should be sure that your child can tell you directly if he really needs more attention from you. This type of communication is important for all children, though the message may vary according to the child's overall communication level. For example, a young child might say (or use an equivalent picture to say), "Come play with me!" If you are concerned that your child may ask too often, then you can limit the number of requests by using a count-down visual system. For example, you may give him five "play with me" cards to use for a holiday party. Children with more sophisticated communication skills can be taught to say, "I know you're busy but can we do something together soon? I'm getting a bit anxious!"

Review

In this chapter, we have used examples of routines that your family may use at home, in your neighborhood, and in the general community. All of the ideas that we have introduced via the Pyramid Approach now become integrated to best help your child with autism effectively cope with many different situations. To successfully teach your child in these varied settings, you must focus on functional activities using powerful rewards (as natural as possible) while assuring that your child has a set of critical functional communication skills (regardless of the modality he uses to communicate). In addition, you must handle any problematic behaviors by first addressing their cause and then identifying appropriate replacement skills.

Conclusion

After reading the preceding chapters, you should understand how to decide upon the type of lesson involved within any activity. You should be able to choose a teaching strategy to match that lesson and later promote its expansion into other settings. You should also understand the importance of responding to your child's errors in a planned and consistent manner. Finally, you should now know how to collect information that will help you decide whether your teaching plans have been successful or whether you need to make some adjustments.

At this point, you should have the knowledge you need to teach your child with autism in many settings and circumstances. When you encounter problems and challenges, you can return to the elements of the Pyramid Approach to find a potential solution in a systematic fashion. We know that you will feel great pride as you watch the growth of your child in and around your home!

Forms & Checklists

AREAS OF THE HOME AND COMMON ACTIVITIES

Area of home/apartment	Common activities
Kitchen	
Living room	
Dining room	
Child's bedroom	
Parent's bedroom	

Rec/TV room	
Laundry area	
Garage	
Basement	
Other	

COMMUNICATION PROGRAMMING ACROSS THE DAY© (for Home Use)

Child: ______________________ Date: ______________

Time	Activity	Location	Functional Goals	Expressive Skills	Direction Following
2:45	Arrival Free time	Doorway Bathroom	Unload book bags Toileting Free play	Request help/toy Answer "Do you want?"	Follow simple directions: "Go to bathroom" "Give it to me"
3:00	Snack	Kitchen	Eat properly/ set-clean table Social interaction Communication Direction-following	Request: snacks/drink/ utensils Request items to complete setting table Answer "What do you see?" Answer "Do you want?"	Respond to directions: "Get…"(spoon, cup, plate, snack items, drink, straw) "Put in/on…" (sink, garbage, table, counter)
3:30	Play	Backyard or basement	Transition to play area Gross motor: ■kick/throw ball ■run/jump ■build with blocks	Request desired toy/area Request help Comment on environment	Respond to "kick" vs. "throw" Respond to "run" vs. "jump" Respond to "select block by color, size OR shape"

4:15	Wash, Laundry	Bathroom Laundry area	Transition to bathroom then laundry Wash hands/face Put wash in Take out of dryer	Request desired item Ask for help Answer "Do you need?" Comment on type, color, and size of clothes	"Throw away" "Give me the [type of clothes]" "Put color/size/type here" "Push start button"
4:45	Watch TV/Video	Den	Turn on TV, DVD, put in disc Comment about movie	Request DVD Request "help" Signal "all done" Comment on actions of characters Politely say "no thanks" to "Let's watch X"	"Please turn the volume up/down" "What is she doing?" "What is her name?"

COMMUNICATION PROGRAMMING ACROSS THE DAY© (for Home Use)

Child: ______________________________ Date: ______________

Time	Activity	Location	Functional Goals	Expressive Skills	Direction Following

ROUTINES AND COMMUNICATION IN THE HOME WORKSHEET©

Summary of Routines

Time of Day: MORNING			
Routine	**Reinforcement (routine itself or finishing routine)**	**Area of House/Class**	**Materials**
get dressed	finishing—gets 5 minutes of video	bedroom	underwear, pants, shirt, socks, shoes
wash hands	finishing—gets breakfast	bathroom	water, soap, towel
eat breakfast	routine is reinforcing	kitchen	cereal, bowl, milk, spoon
brush teeth	finishing—gets 5 minutes of free play	bathroom	water, toothbrush, toothpaste, towel

get ready for bus	finishing—likes to ride school bus	family room	shoes, coat, backpack

ROUTINES AND COMMUNICATION IN THE HOME WORKSHEET©

Summary of Routines

Time of Day: AFTERNOON			
Routine	**Reinforcement (routine itself or finishing routine)**	**Area of House/Class**	**Materials**
arriving—take coat off, hang coat, unload book bag, shoes off	finishing—gets snack	family room	hanger/hook
snack	routine—likes to eat snack	kitchen	favorite foods, plate, cup,
coat/shoes on	finishing—gets to go outside	family room	coat, shoes
outdoor play	routine—likes to play outside	back yard	swings, ball

coming in—coat off, shoes off	finishing—gets to watch video	family room	hanger/hook
video	routine—likes videos	family room	television, video, favorite chair/ mat, etc.
wash hands	finishing—dinner is next	bathroom	water, soap, towel
dinner	routine—eats favorite foods	kitchen	plate, cup, bowl, utensils, food

ROUTINES AND COMMUNICATION IN THE HOME WORKSHEET©

Summary of Routines

Time of Day: EVENING			
Routine	**Reinforcement (routine itself or finishing routine)**	**Area of House/Class**	**Materials**
help with dishes	finishing—gets to take bath next	kitchen	refrigerator, dishwasher
bath time	routine—loves bubble baths	bathroom	water, bubbles, washcloth, toys, towel
pajamas on	finishing—gets to watch video	bedroom	pajamas
video	routine	family room	television, video, favorite chair

brush teeth	finishing—gets to play before bed	bathroom	water, toothbrush, toothpaste, towel
bed time	routine—likes to look at books in bed	bedroom	books, bed, lamp

ROUTINES AND COMMUNICATION IN THE HOME WORKSHEET©

Summary of Routines

Time of Day: MORNING			
Routine	Reinforcement (routine itself or finishing routine)	Area of House/Class	Materials

ROUTINES AND COMMUNICATION IN THE HOME WORKSHEET©

Summary of Routines

Time of Day: AFTERNOON			
Routine	Reinforcement (routine itself or finishing routine)	Area of House/Class	Materials

ROUTINES AND COMMUNICATION IN THE HOME WORKSHEET©

Summary of Routines

Time of Day: EVENING			
Routine	Reinforcement (routine itself or finishing routine)	Area of House/Class	Materials

ROUTINES AND COMMUNICATION IN THE HOME WORKSHEET©

Steps within Routines

Routine	Steps	Vocabulary for Requesting
eating snack—cookies and milk on table	1. go to kitchen	1. ________
	2. get cup	2. cup
	3. get plate	3. plate
	4. put on table	4. ________
	5. sit down	5. ________
Sabotage strategy once routine is mastered:	6. open bag of cookies	6. cookies
vary: have no cup available; have no plates available; no cookies or wrong cookies on table; no milk available; milk carton sealed	7. put two cookies on plate	7. ________
	8. open milk	8. milk
	9. pour milk	9. help
	10. eat cookies	10. ________
	11. drink milk	11. ________
	12. clean up	12. ________
	Reinforcement: access to cookies and milk	

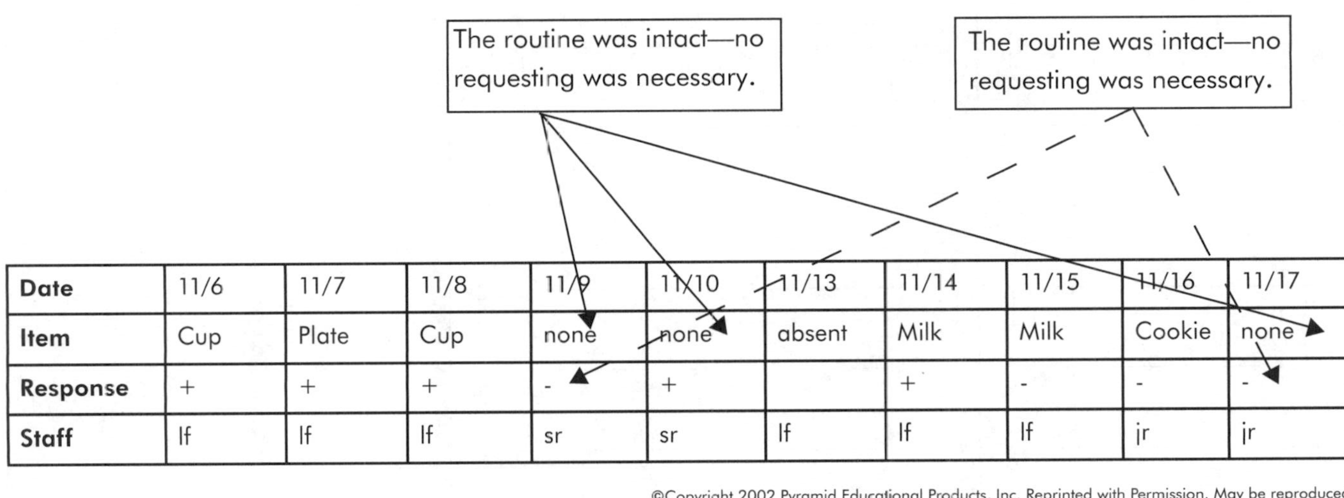

Date	11/6	11/7	11/8	11/9	11/10	11/13	11/14	11/15	11/16	11/17
Item	Cup	Plate	Cup	none	none	absent	Milk	Milk	Cookie	none
Response	+	+	+	-	+		+	-	-	-
Staff	lf	lf	lf	sr	sr	lf	lf	lf	jr	jr

ROUTINES AND COMMUNICATION IN THE HOME WORKSHEET©

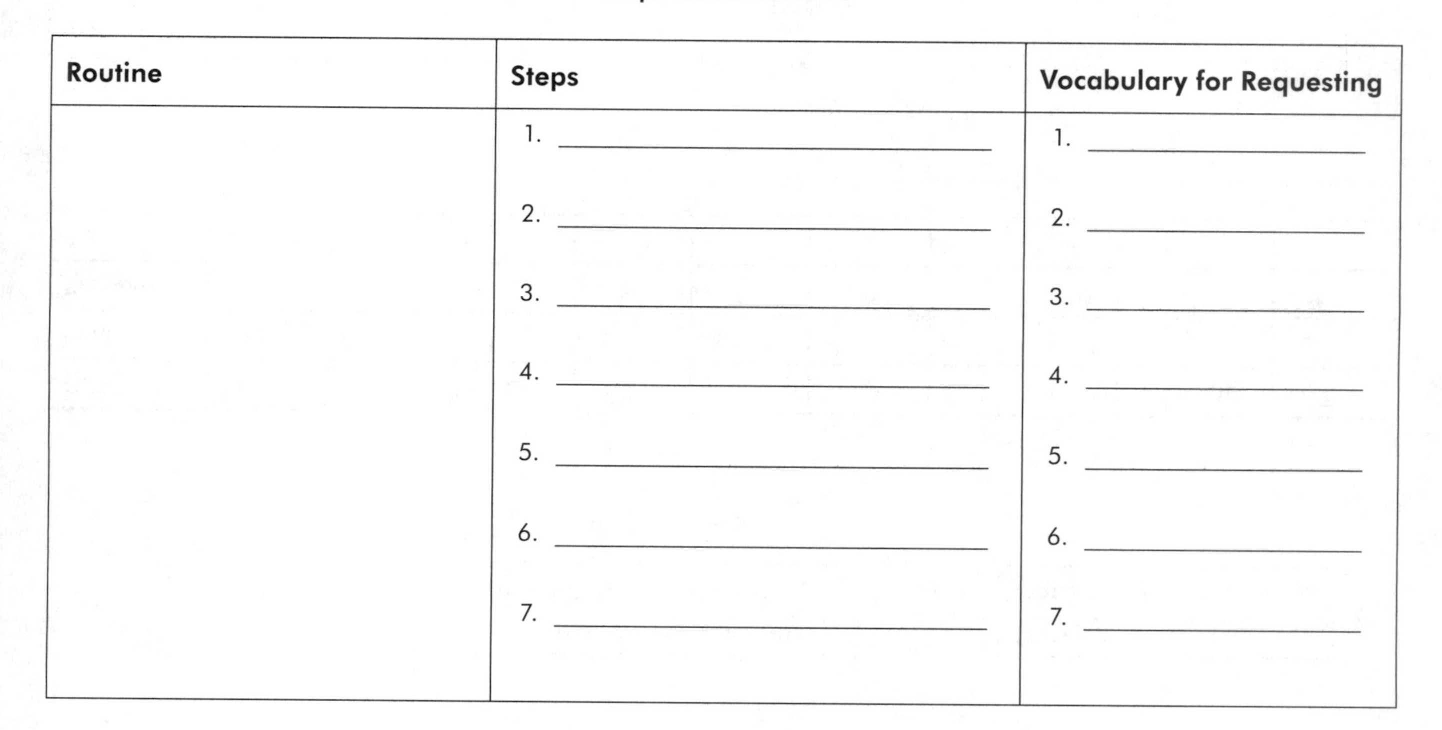

Steps within Routines

Routine	Steps	Vocabulary for Requesting
	1. ______	1. ______
	2. ______	2. ______
	3. ______	3. ______
	4. ______	4. ______
	5. ______	5. ______
	6. ______	6. ______
	7. ______	7. ______

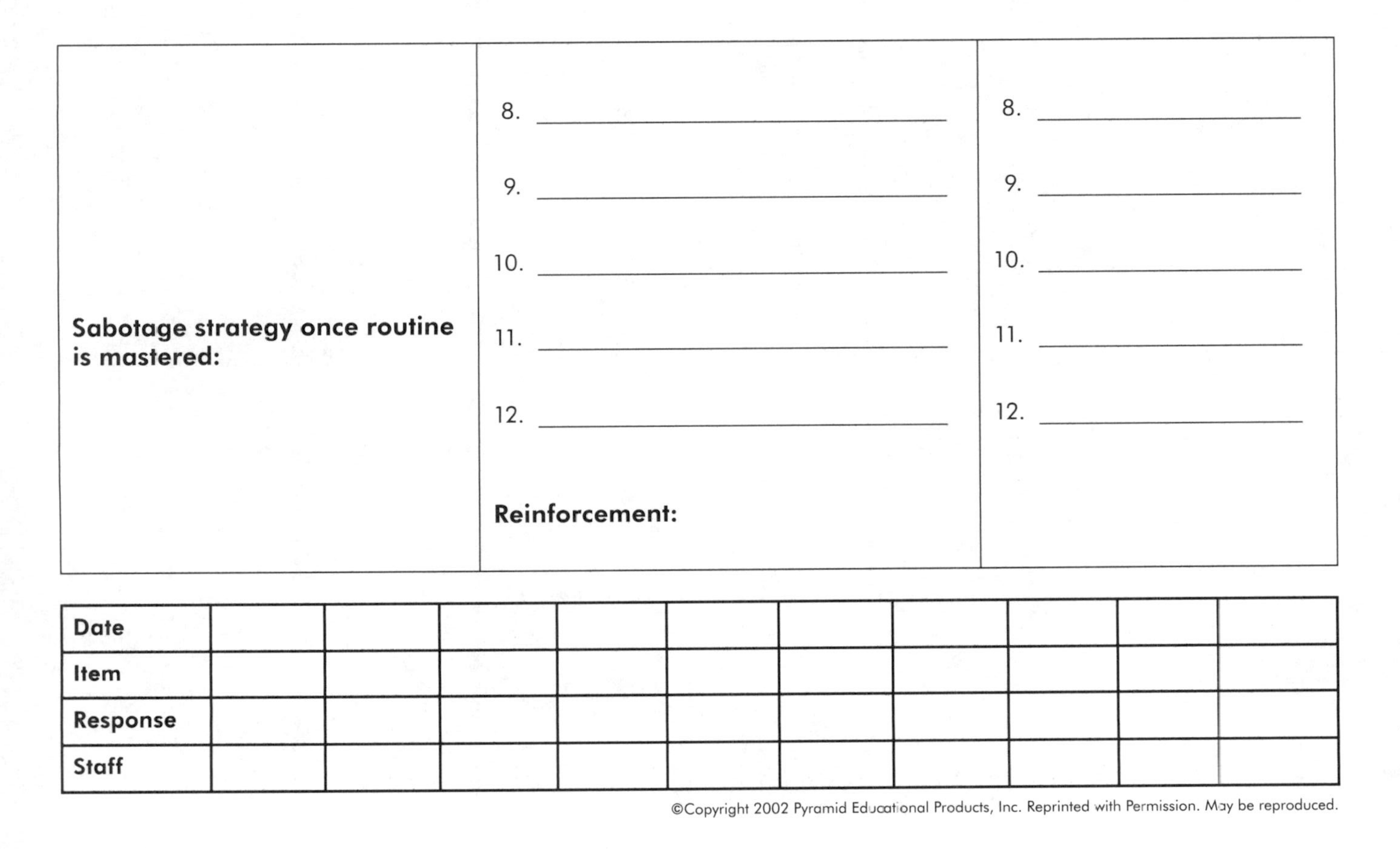

Sabotage strategy once routine is mastered:	8. ____ 9. ____ 10. ____ 11. ____ 12. ____ **Reinforcement:**	8. ____ 9. ____ 10. ____ 11. ____ 12. ____

Date										
Item										
Response										
Staff										

Bibliography

Anderson, S. et al. (2007). *Self-Help Skills for People with Autism: A Systematic Teaching Approach.* Bethesda, MD: Woodbine House.

Bondy, A. & Frost, L. (2002). *A Picture's Worth: PECS and Other Visual Communication Strategies in Autism.* Bethesda, MD: Woodbine House, Inc.

Bondy, A. & Sulzer-Azaroff, B. (2002). *The Pyramid Approach to Education in Autism,* 2nd Edition. Newark, DE: Pyramid Products, Inc.

Cafiero, J. (2005). *Meaningful Exchanges for People with Autism: An Introduction to Augmentative & Alternative Communication.* Bethesda, MD: Woodbine House.

Charlop-Christy, M. H., & Daneshvar, S. (2003). Using video modeling to teach perspective taking to children with autism. *Journal of Positive Behavior Interventions, 5* 12-21.

Delmolino, L. & Harris, S. (2005). *Incentives for Change: Motivating People with Autism Spectrum Disorders to Learn and Gain Independence.* Bethesda, MD: Woodbine House.

Glasberg, B. (2006). *Functional Behavior Assessment for People with Autism: Making Sense of Seemingly Senseless Behavior.* Bethesda, MD: Woodbine House.

Glennen, S.L. & DeCoste, D. (1997). *The Handbook of Augmentative and Alternative Communication.* San Diego: Singular Publishing Group.

Harris, S. & Weiss, M. (2007). *Right from the Start: Behavioral Intervention for Young Children with Autism.* 2nd ed. Bethesda, MD: Woodbine House.

Mirenda, P. (2002). Augmentative and alternative communications systems. In A. Bondy & L. Frost, *A Picture's Worth: PECS and Other Visual Communication Strategies in Autism* (pp. 43-66). Bethesda, MD: Woodbine House.

Mirenda, P. (2003). Toward functional augmentative and alternative communication for students with autism: Manual signs, graphic symbols, and voice output communication aids. *Language, Speech, and Hearing Services in Schools,* 34, 203-216.

Skinner, B. F. (1957). *Verbal Behavior.* Englewood Cliffs, NJ: Prentice-Hall.

Sulzer-Azaroff, B., Fleming, R. & Mashikian, S., (2003). *Study Questions, Laboratory, and Field Activities to Accompany the Pyramid Approach to Education in Autism.* Newark, DE: Pyramid Products, Inc.

Weiss, M. & Harris, S. (2001). *Reaching Out, Joining In: Teaching Social Skills to Young Children with Autism.* Bethesda, MD: Woodbine House.

Wert, B. Y., & Neisworth, J. T. (2003). Effects of video self-modeling on spontaneous requesting in children with autism. *Journal of Positive Behavior Interventions, 5,* 30-34.

Index

About the Authors

Andy Bondy, Ph.D., has over 35 years experience working with children and adults with autism and related developmental disabilities. For more than a dozen years he served as the Director of the Statewide Delaware Autistic Program. He and his wife, Lori Frost, pioneered the development of the Picture Exchange Communication System (PECS). Based upon principles described in B.F. Skinner's *Verbal Behavior*, the system gradually moves from relatively simple yet spontaneous manding to tacting with multiple attributes. He designed the *Pyramid Approach to Education* as a comprehensive combination of broad-spectrum behavior analysis and functional communication strategies. He is the co-founder of Pyramid Educational Consultants, Inc., an internationally based team of specialists from many fields who annually train and act as consultants for thousands of people around the world.

Lori A. Frost, M.S., CCC/SLP, is a speech/language pathologist certified by the American Speech-Language-Hearing Association. She has over 25 years experience working with children with limited communication and severely challenging behavior. She is co-developer of the Picture Exchange Communication System and coauthor of the *PECS Training Manual, 2nd edition*. Ms. Frost is cofounder of Pyramid Educational Consultants, Inc. She has led regional, national, and international conferences and workshops. She consults to numerous schools and programs worldwide regarding the development of functional communication skills for children and adults with autism and related disabilities.